Designing Distributed Systems

Patterns and Paradigms for Scalable, Reliable Services

Brendan Burns

Beijing · Boston · Farnham · Sebastopol · Tokyo

Designing Distributed Systems

by Brendan Burns

Published by O'Reilly Media, Inc., 1005 Gravenstein Highway North, Sebastopol, CA 95472.

O'Reilly books may be purchased for educational, business, or sales promotional use. Online editions are also available for most titles (*http://oreilly.com/safari*). For more information, contact our corporate/institutional sales department: 800-998-9938 or *corporate@oreilly.com*.

Editor: Angela Rufino	**Indexer:** WordCo Indexing Services, Inc.
Production Editor: Colleen Cole	**Interior Designer:** David Futato
Copyeditor: Gillian McGarvey	**Cover Designer:** Randy Comer
Proofreader: Christina Edwards	**Illustrator:** Rebecca Demarest

February 2018:   First Edition

Revision History for the First Edition
2018-02-20:   First Release
2018-12-14:   Second Release

See *http://oreilly.com/catalog/errata.csp?isbn=9781491983645* for release details.

978-1-491-98364-5

[LSI]

Table of Contents

Part II.   Serving Patterns

Part III. Batch Computational Patterns

Preface

Who Should Read This Book

At this point, nearly every developer is a developer or consumer (or both) of distributed systems. Even relatively simple mobile applications are backed with cloud APIs so that their data can be present on whatever device the customer happens to be using. Whether you are new to developing distributed systems or an expert with scars on your hands to prove it, the patterns and components described in this book can transform your development of distributed systems from art to science. Reusable components and patterns for distributed systems will enable you to focus on the core details of your application. This book will help any developer become better, faster, and more efficient at building distributed systems.

Why I Wrote This Book

Throughout my career as a developer of a variety of software systems from web search to the cloud, I have built a large number of scalable, reliable distributed systems. Each of these systems was, by and large, built from scratch. In general, this is true of all distributed applications. Despite having many of the same concepts and even at times nearly identical logic, the ability to apply patterns or reuse components is often very, very challenging. This forced me to waste time reimplementing systems, and each system ended up less polished than it might have otherwise been.

The recent introduction of containers and container orchestrators fundamentally changed the landscape of distributed system development. Suddenly we have an object and interface for expressing core distributed system patterns and building reusable containerized components. I wrote this book to bring together all of the practitioners of distributed systems, giving us a shared language and common standard library so that we can all build better systems more quickly.

The World of Distributed Systems Today

Once upon a time, people wrote programs that ran on one machine and were also accessed from that machine. The world has changed. Now, nearly every application is a *distributed system* running on multiple machines and accessed by multiple users from all over the world. Despite their prevalence, the design and development of these systems is often a black art practiced by a select group of wizards. But as with everything in technology, the world of distributed systems is advancing, regularizing, and abstracting. In this book I capture a collection of repeatable, generic patterns that can make the development of reliable distributed systems more approachable and efficient. The adoption of patterns and reusable components frees developers from reimplementing the same systems over and over again. This time is then freed to focus on building the core application itself.

Navigating This Book

This book is organized into a 4 parts as follows:

Chapter 1, Introduction
> Introduces distributed systems and explains why patterns and reusable components can make such a difference in the rapid development of reliable distributed systems.

Part I, Single-Node Patterns
> Chapters 2 through 4 discuss reusable patterns and components that occur on individual nodes within a distributed system. It covers the side-car, adapter, and ambassador single-node patterns.

Part II, Serving Patterns
> Chapters 8 and 9 cover multi-node distributed patterns for long-running serving systems like web applications. Patterns for replicating, scaling, and master election are discussed.

Part III, Batch Computational Patterns
> Chapters 10 through 12 cover distributed system patterns for large-scale batch data processing covering work queues, event-based processing, and coordinated workflows.

If you are an experienced distributed systems engineer, you can likely skip the first couple of chapters, though you may want to skim them to understand how we expect these patterns to be applied and why we think the general notion of distributed system patterns is so important.

Everyone will likely find utility in the single-node patterns as they are the most generic and most reusable patterns in the book.

Depending on your goals and the systems you are interested in developing, you can choose to focus on either large-scale big data patterns, or patterns for long-running servers (or both). The two parts are largely independent from each other and can be read in any order.

Likewise, if you have extensive distributed system experience, you may find that some of the early patterns chapters (e.g., Part II on naming, discovery, and load balancing) are redundant with what you already know, so feel free to skim through to gain the high-level insights—but don't forget to look at all of the pretty pictures!

Conventions Used in This Book

The following typographical conventions are used in this book:

Italic
> Indicates new terms, URLs, email addresses, filenames, and file extensions.

`Constant width`
> Used for program listings, as well as within paragraphs to refer to program elements such as variable or function names, databases, data types, environment variables, statements, and keywords.

`Constant width bold`
> Shows commands or other text that should be typed literally by the user.

`Constant width italic`
> Shows text that should be replaced with user-supplied values or by values determined by context.

 This icon signifies a tip, suggestion, or general note.

 This icon indicates a warning or caution.

Online Resources

Though this book describes generally applicable distributed system patterns, it expects that readers are familiar with containers and container orchestration systems.

If you don't have a lot of pre-existing knowledge about these things, we recommend the following resources:

- *https://docker.io*
- *https://kubernetes.io*
- *https://dcos.io*

Using Code Examples

Supplemental material (code examples, exercises, etc.) is available for download at *https://github.com/brendandburns/designing-distributed-systems*.

This book is here to help you get your job done. In general, if example code is offered with this book, you may use it in your programs and documentation. You do not need to contact us for permission unless you're reproducing a significant portion of the code. For example, writing a program that uses several chunks of code from this book does not require permission. Selling or distributing a CD-ROM of examples from O'Reilly books does require permission. Answering a question by citing this book and quoting example code does not require permission. Incorporating a significant amount of example code from this book into your product's documentation does require permission.

We appreciate, but do not require, attribution. An attribution usually includes the title, author, publisher, and ISBN. For example: "*Designing Distributed Systems* by Brendan Burns (O'Reilly). Copyright 2018 Brendan Burns, 978-1-491-98364-5."

If you feel your use of code examples falls outside fair use or the permission given above, feel free to contact us at *permissions@oreilly.com*.

O'Reilly Safari

Safari (formerly Safari Books Online) is a membership-based training and reference platform for enterprise, government, educators, and individuals.

Members have access to thousands of books, training videos, Learning Paths, interactive tutorials, and curated playlists from over 250 publishers, including O'Reilly Media, Harvard Business Review, Prentice Hall Professional, Addison-Wesley Professional, Microsoft Press, Sams, Que, Peachpit Press, Adobe, Focal Press, Cisco Press, John Wiley & Sons, Syngress, Morgan Kaufmann, IBM Redbooks, Packt, Adobe Press, FT Press, Apress, Manning, New Riders, McGraw-Hill, Jones & Bartlett, and Course Technology, among others.

For more information, please visit *http://oreilly.com/safari*.

How to Contact Us

Please address comments and questions concerning this book to the publisher:

O'Reilly Media, Inc.
1005 Gravenstein Highway North
Sebastopol, CA 95472
800-998-9938 (in the United States or Canada)
707-829-0515 (international or local)
707-829-0104 (fax)

We have a web page for this book, where we list errata, examples, and any additional information. You can access this page at *http://bit.ly/designing-distributed-systems*.

To comment or ask technical questions about this book, send email to *bookquestions@oreilly.com*.

For more information about our books, courses, conferences, and news, see our website at *http://www.oreilly.com*.

Find us on Facebook: *http://facebook.com/oreilly*

Follow us on Twitter: *http://twitter.com/oreillymedia*

Watch us on YouTube: *http://www.youtube.com/oreillymedia*

Acknowledgments

I'd like to thank my wife Robin and my children for everything they do to keep me happy and sane. To all of the people along the way who took the time to help me learn all of these things, many thanks! Also thanks to my parents for that first SE/30.

Introduction

Today's world of always-on applications and APIs have availability and reliability requirements that would have been required of only a handful of mission critical services around the globe only a few decades ago. Likewise, the potential for rapid, viral growth of a service means that every application has to be built to scale nearly instantly in response to user demand. These constraints and requirements mean that almost every application that is built—whether it is a consumer mobile app or a back-end payments application—needs to be a distributed system.

But building distributed systems is challenging. Often, they are one-off bespoke solutions. In this way, distributed system development bears a striking resemblance to the world of software development prior to the development of modern object-oriented programming languages. Fortunately, as with the development of object-oriented languages, there have been technological advances that have dramatically reduced the challenges of building distributed systems. In this case, it is the rising popularity of containers and container orchestrators. As with the concept of objects within object-oriented programming, these containerized building blocks are the basis for the development of reusable components and patterns that dramatically simplify and make accessible the practices of building reliable distributed systems. In the following introduction, we give a brief history of the developments that have led to where we are today.

A Brief History of Systems Development

In the beginning, there were machines built for specific purposes, such as calculating artillery tables or the tides, breaking codes, or other precise, complicated but rote mathematical applications. Eventually these purpose-built machines evolved into general-purpose programmable machines. And eventually they evolved from running one program at a time to running multiple programs on a single machine via time-sharing operating systems, but these machines were still disjoint from each other.

Gradually, machines came to be networked together, and client-server architectures were born so that a relatively low-powered machine on someone's desk could be used to harness the greater power of a mainframe in another room or building. While this sort of client-server programming was somewhat more complicated than writing a program for a single machine, it was still fairly straightforward to understand. The client(s) made requests; the server(s) serviced those requests.

In the early 2000s, the rise of the internet and large-scale datacenters consisting of thousands of relatively low-cost commodity computers networked together gave rise to the widespread development of *distributed systems*. Unlike client-server architectures, distributed system applications are made up of multiple different applications running on different machines, or many replicas running across different machines, all communicating together to implement a system like web-search or a retail sales platform.

Because of their distributed nature, when structured properly, distributed systems are inherently more reliable. And when architected correctly, they can lead to much more scalable organizational models for the teams of software engineers that built these systems. Unfortunately, these advantages come at a cost. These distributed systems can be significantly more complicated to design, build, and debug correctly. The engineering skills needed to build a reliable distributed system are significantly higher than those needed to build single-machine applications like mobile or web frontends. Regardless, the need for reliable distributed systems only continues to grow. Thus there is a corresponding need for the tools, patterns, and practices for building them.

Fortunately, technology has also increased the ease with which you can build distributed systems. Containers, container images, and container orchestrators have all become popular in recent years because they are the foundation and building blocks for reliable distributed systems. Using containers and container orchestration as a foundation, we can establish a collection of patterns and reusable components. These patterns and components are a toolkit that we can use to build our systems more reliably and efficiently.

A Brief History of Patterns in Software Development

This is not the first time such a transformation has occurred in the software industry. For a better context on how patterns, practices, and reusable components have previously reshaped systems development, it is helpful to look at past moments when similar transformations have taken place.

Formalization of Algorithmic Programming

Though people had been programming for more than a decade before its publication in 1962, Donald Knuth's collection, *The Art of Computer Programming* (Addison-Wesley Professional), marks an important chapter in the development of computer science. In particular, the books contain algorithms not designed for any specific computer, but rather to educate the reader on the algorithms themselves. These algorithms then could be adapted to the specific architecture of the machine being used or the specific problem that the reader was solving. This formalization was important because it provided users with a shared toolkit for building their programs, but also because it showed that there was a general-purpose concept that programmers should learn and then subsequently apply in a variety of different contexts. The algorithms themselves, independent of any specific problem to solve, were worth understanding for their own sake.

Patterns for Object-Oriented Programming

Knuth's books represent an important landmark in the thinking about computer programming, and algorithms represent an important component in the development of computer programming. However, as the complexity of programs grew, and the number of people writing a single program grew from the single digits to the double digits and eventually to the thousands, it became clear that procedural programming languages and algorithms were insufficient for the tasks of modern-day programming. These changes in computer programming led to the development of object-oriented programming languages, which elevated data, reusability, and extensibility to peers of the algorithm in the development of computer programs.

In response to these changes to computer programming, there were changes to the patterns and practices for programming as well. Throughout the early to mid-1990s, there was an explosion of books on patterns for object-oriented programming. The most famous of these is the "gang of four" book, *Design Patterns: Elements of Reusable Object-Oriented Programming* by Erich Gamma et al. (Addison-Wesley Professional). *Design Patterns* gave a common language and framework to the task of programming. It described a series of interface-based patterns that could be reused in a variety of contexts. Because of advances in object-oriented programming and specifically interfaces, these patterns could also be implemented as generic reusable libraries. These libraries could be written once by a community of developers and reused repeatedly, saving time and improving reliability.

The Rise of Open Source Software

Though the concept of developers sharing source code has been around nearly since the beginning of computing, and formal free software organizations have been in existence since the mid-1980s, the very late 1990s and the 2000s saw a dramatic increase in the development and distribution of open source software. Though open source is only tangentially related to the development of patterns for distributed systems, it is important in the sense that it was through the open source communities that it became increasingly clear that software development in general and distributed systems development in particular are community endeavors. It is important to note that all of the container technology that forms the foundation of the patterns described in this book has been developed and released as open source software. The value of patterns for both describing and improving the practice of distributed development is especially clear when you look at it from this community perspective.

 What is a pattern for a distributed system? There are plenty of instructions out there that will tell you how to install specific distributed systems (such as a NoSQL database). Likewise, there are recipes for a specific collection of systems (like a MEAN stack). But when I speak of patterns, I'm referring to general blueprints for organizing distributed systems, without mandating any specific technology or application choices. The purpose of a pattern is to provide general advice or structure to guide your design. The hope is that such patterns will guide your thinking and also be generally applicable to a wide variety of applications and environments.

The Value of Patterns, Practices, and Components

Before spending any of your valuable time reading about a series of patterns that I claim will improve your development practices, teach you new skills, and—let's face it —change your life, it's reasonable to ask: "Why?" What is it about the design patterns and practices that can change the way that we design and build software? In this section, I'll lay out the reasons I think this is an important topic, and hopefully convince you to stick with me for the rest of the book.

Standing on the Shoulders of Giants

As a starting point, the value that patterns for distributed systems offer is the opportunity to figuratively stand on the shoulders of giants. It's rarely the case that the problems we solve or the systems we build are truly unique. Ultimately, the combination of pieces that we put together and the overall business model that the software enables may be something that the world has never seen before. But the way the system is built and the problems it encounters as it aspires to be reliable, agile, and scalable are not new.

This, then, is the first value of patterns: they allow us to learn from the mistakes of others. Perhaps you have never built a distributed system before, or perhaps you have never built this type of distributed system. Rather than hoping that a colleague has some experience in this area or learning by making the same mistakes that others have already made, you can turn to patterns as your guide. Learning about patterns for distributed system development is the same as learning about any other best practice in computer programming. It accelerates your ability to build software without requiring that you have direct experience with the systems, mistakes, and firsthand learning that led to the codification of the pattern in the first place.

A Shared Language for Discussing Our Practice

Learning about and accelerating our understanding of distributed systems is only the first value of having a shared set of patterns. Patterns have value even for experienced distributed system developers who already understand them well. Patterns provide a shared vocabulary that enables us to understand each other quickly. This understanding forms the basis for knowledge sharing and further learning.

To better understand this, imagine that we both are using the same object to build our house. I call that object a "Foo" while you call that object a "Bar." How long will we spend arguing about the value of a Foo versus that of a Bar, or trying to explain the differing properties of Foo and Bar until we figure out that we're speaking about the same object? Only once we determine that Foo and Bar are the same can we truly start learning from each other's experience.

Without a common vocabulary, we waste time in arguments of "violent agreement" or in explaining concepts that others understand but know by another name. Consequently, another significant value of patterns is to provide a common set of names and definitions so that we don't waste time worrying about naming, and instead get right down to discussing the details and implementation of the core concepts.

I have seen this happen in my short time working on containers. Along the way, the notion of a *sidecar* container (described in Chapter 2 of this book) took hold within the container community. Because of this, we no longer have to spend time defining what it means to be a sidecar and can instead jump immediately to how the concept can be used to solve a particular problem. "If we just use a sidecar" … "Yeah, and I know just the container we can use for that." This example leads to the third value of patterns: the construction of reusable components.

Shared Components for Easy Reuse

Beyond enabling people to learn from others and providing a shared vocabulary for discussing the art of building systems, patterns provide another important tool for computer programming: the ability to identify common components that can be implemented once.

If we had to create all of the code that our programs use ourselves, we would never get done. Indeed, we would barely get started. Today, every system ever written stands on the shoulders of thousands if not hundreds of thousands of years of human effort. Code for operating systems, printer drivers, distributed databases, container runtimes, and container orchestrators—indeed, the entirety of applications that we build today are built with reusable shared libraries and components.

Patterns are the basis for the definition and development of such reusable components. The formalization of algorithms led to reusable implementations of sorting and other canonical algorithms. The identification of interface-based patterns gave rise to a collection of generic, object-oriented libraries implementing those patterns.

Identifying core patterns for distributed systems enables us to to build shared common components. Implementing these patterns as container images with HTTP-based interfaces means they can be reused across many different programming languages. And, of course, building reusable components improves the quality of each component because the shared code base gets sufficient usage to identify bugs and weaknesses, and sufficient attention to ensure that they get fixed.

Summary

Distributed systems are required to implement the level of reliability, agility, and scale expected of modern computer programs. Distributed system design continues to be more of a black art practiced by wizards than a science applied by laypeople. The identification of common patterns and practices has regularized and improved the practice of algorithmic development and object-oriented programming. It is this book's goal to do the same for distributed systems. Enjoy!

## PART I

Single-Node Patterns

This book concerns itself with distributed systems, which are applications made up of many different components running on many different machines. However, the first section of this book is devoted to patterns that exist on a single node. The motivation for this is straightforward. Containers are the foundational building block for the patterns in this book, but in the end, groups of containers co-located on a single machine make up the atomic elements of distributed system patterns.

Motivations

Though it is clear as to why you might want to break your distributed application into a collection of different containers running on different machines, it is perhaps somewhat less clear as to why you might also want to break up the components running on a single machine into different containers. To understand the motivation for these groups of containers, it is worth considering the goals behind containerization. In general, the goal of a container is to establish boundaries around specific resources (e.g., this application needs two cores and 8 GB of memory). Likewise, the boundary delineates team ownership (e.g., this team owns this image). Finally, the boundary is intended to provide separation of concerns (e.g., this image does this one thing).

All of these reasons provide motivation for splitting up an application on a single machine into a group of containers. Consider resource isolation first. Your application may be made up of two components: one is a user-facing application server and the other is a background configuration file loader. Clearly, end-user-facing request latency is the highest priority, so the user-facing application needs to have sufficient resources to ensure that it is highly responsive. On the other hand, the background configuration loader is mostly a best-effort service; if it is delayed slightly during times of high user-request volume, the system will be okay. Likewise, the background configuration loader should not impact the quality of service that end users receive. For all of these reasons, you want to separate the user-facing service and the background shard loader into different containers. This allows you to attach different resource requirements and priorities to the two different containers and, for example, ensure that the background loader opportunistically steals cycles from the user-facing service whenever it is lightly loaded and the cycles are free. Likewise, separate resource requirements for the two containers ensure that the background loader will be terminated before the user-facing service if there is a resource contention issue caused by a memory leak or other overcommitment of memory resources.

In addition to this resource isolation, there are other reasons to split your single-node application into multiple containers. Consider the task of scaling a team. There is good reason to believe that the ideal team size is six to eight people. In order to structure teams in this manner and yet still build significant systems, we need to have small, focused pieces for each team to own. Additionally, often some of the components, if factored properly, are reusable modules that can be used by many teams. Consider, for example, the task of keeping a local filesystem synchronized with a git source code repository. If you build this Git sync tool as a separate container, you can reuse it with PHP, HTML, JavaScript, Python, and numerous other web-serving environments. If you instead factor each environment as a single container where, for example, the Python runtime and the Git synchronization are inextricably bound, then this sort of modular reuse (and the corresponding small team that owns that reusable module) are impossible.

Finally, even if your application is small and all of your containers are owned by a single team, the separation of concerns ensures that your application is well understood and can easily be tested, updated, and deployed. Small, focused applications are easier to understand and have fewer couplings to other systems. This means, for example, that you can deploy the Git synchronization container without having to also redeploy your application server. This leads to rollouts with fewer dependencies and smaller scope. That, in turn, leads to more reliable rollouts (and rollbacks), which leads to greater agility and flexibility when deploying your application.

Summary

I hope that all of these examples have motivated you to think about breaking up your applications, even those on a single node, into multiple containers. The following chapters describe some patterns that can help guide you as you build modular groups of containers. In contrast to multi-node, distributed patterns, all of these patterns assume tight dependencies among all of the containers in the pattern. In particular, they assume that all of the containers in the pattern can be reliably coscheduled onto a single machine. They also assume that all of the containers in the pattern can optionally share volumes or parts of their filesystems as well as other key container resources like network namespaces and shared memory. This tight grouping is called a *pod* in Kubernetes,[1] but the concept is generally applicable to different container orchestrators, though some support it more natively than others.

---

1 Kubernetes (*https://kubernetes.io/*) is an open source system for automating deployment, scaling, and management of containerized applications. Check out my book, *Kubernetes: Up and Running* (O'Reilly).

## CHAPTER 2

The Sidecar Pattern

The first single-node pattern is the sidecar pattern. The sidecar pattern is a single-node pattern made up of two containers. The first is the *application container*. It contains the core logic for the application. Without this container, the application would not exist. In addition to the application container, there is a *sidecar container*. The role of the sidecar is to augment and improve the application container, often without the application container's knowledge. In its simplest form, a sidecar container can be used to add functionality to a container that might otherwise be difficult to improve. Sidecar containers are coscheduled onto the same machine via an atomic *container group*, such as the pod API object in Kubernetes. In addition to being scheduled on the same machine, the application container and sidecar container share a number of resources, including parts of the filesystem, hostname and network, and many other namespaces. A generic image of this sidecar pattern is shown in Figure 2-1.

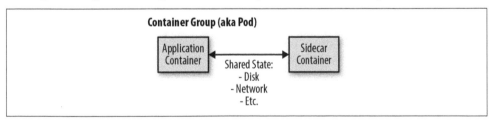

Figure 2-1. The generic sidecar pattern

An Example Sidecar: Adding HTTPS to a Legacy Service

Consider, for example, a legacy web service. Years ago, when it was built, internal network security was not as high a priority for the company, and thus, the application only services requests over unencrypted HTTP, not HTTPS. Due to recent security incidents, the company has mandated the use of HTTPS for all company websites. To compound the misery of the team sent to update this particular web service, the source code for this application was built with an old version of the company's build system, which no longer functions. Containerizing this HTTP application is simple enough: the binary can run in a container with a version of an old Linux distribution on top of a more modern kernel being run by the team's container orchestrator. However, the task of adding HTTPS to this application is significantly more challenging. The team is trying to decide between resurrecting the old build system versus porting the application's source code to the new build system, when one of the team members suggests that they use the sidecar pattern to resolve the situation more easily.

The application of the sidecar pattern to this situation is straightforward. The legacy web service is configured to serve exclusively on localhost (127.0.0.1), which means that only services that share the local network with the server will be able to access the service. Normally, this wouldn't be a practical choice because it would mean that no one could access the web service. However, using the sidecar pattern, in addition to the legacy container, we will add an nginx sidecar container. This nginx container lives in the same network namespace as the legacy web application, so it can access the service that is running on localhost. At the same time, this nginx service can terminate HTTPS traffic on the external IP address of the pod and proxy that traffic to the legacy web application (see Figure 2-2). Since this unencrypted traffic is only sent via the local loopback adapter inside the container group, the network security team is satisfied that the data is safe. Likewise, by using the sidecar pattern, the team has modernized a legacy application without having to figure out how to rebuild a new application to serve HTTPS.

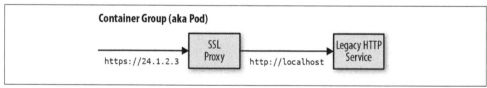

Figure 2-2. The HTTPS sidecar

Dynamic Configuration with Sidecars

Simply proxying traffic into an existing application is not the only use for a sidecar. Another common example is configuration synchronization. Many applications use a configuration file for parameterizing the application; this may be a raw text file or something more structured like XML, JSON, or YAML. Many pre-existing applications were written to assume that this file was present on the filesystem and read their configuration from there. However, in a cloud-native environment it is often quite useful to use an API for updating configuration. This allows you to do a dynamic push of configuration information via an API instead of manually logging in to every server and updating the configuration file using imperative commands. The desire for such an API is driven both by ease of use as well as the ability to add automation like rollback, which makes configuring (and reconfiguring) safer and easier.

Similar to the case of HTTPS, new applications can be written with the expectation that configuration is a dynamic property that should be obtained using a cloud API, but adapting and updating an existing application can be significantly more challenging. Fortunately, the sidecar pattern again can be used to provide new functionality that augments a legacy application without changing the existing application. For the sidecar pattern shown in Figure 2-3, there again are two containers: the container that is the serving application and the container that is the configuration manager. The two containers are grouped together into a pod where they share a directory between themselves. This shared directory is where the configuration file is maintained.

When the legacy application starts, it loads its configuration from the filesystem, as expected. When the configuration manager starts, it examines the configuration API and looks for differences between the local filesystem and the configuration stored in the API. If there are differences, the configuration manager downloads the new configuration to the local filesystem and signals to the legacy application that it should reconfigure itself with this new configuration. The actual mechanism for this notification varies by application. Some applications actually watch the configuration file for changes, while others respond to a SIGHUP signal. In extreme cases, the configuration manager may send a SIGKILL signal to abort the legacy application. Once aborted, the container orchestration system will restart the legacy application, at which point it will load its new configuration. As with adding HTTPS to an existing application, this pattern illustrates how the sidecar pattern can help adapt preexisting applications to more cloud-native scenarios.

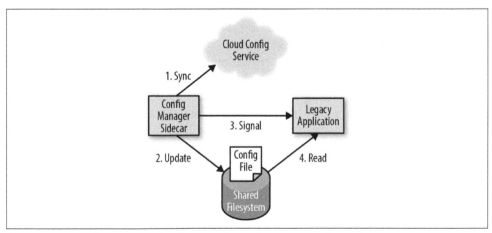

Figure 2-3. A sidecar example of managing a dynamic configuration

Modular Application Containers

At this point, you might be forgiven if you thought that the sole reason for the sidecar pattern to exist was to adapt legacy applications where you no longer wanted to make modifications to the original source code. While this is a common use case for the pattern, there are many other motivations for designing things using sidecars. One of the other main advantages of using the sidecar pattern is modularity and reuse of the components used as sidecars. In deploying any real-world, reliable application, there is functionality that you need for debugging or other management of the application, such as giving a readout of all of the different processes using resources in the container, similar to the top command line tool.

One approach to providing this introspection is to require that each developer implement an HTTP /topz interface that provides a readout of resource usage. To make this easier, you might implement this webhook as a language-specific plugin that the developer could simply link into their application. But even if done this way, the developer would be forced to choose to link it in and your organization would be forced to implement the interface for every language it wants to support. Unless done with extreme rigor, this approach is bound to lead to variations among languages as well as a lack of support for the functionality when using new languages. Instead, this topz functionality can be deployed as a sidecar container that shares the process-id (PID) namespace with the application container. This topz container can introspect all running processes and provide a consistent user interface. Moreover, you can use the orchestration system to automatically add this container to all applications deployed via the orchestration system to ensure that there is a consistent set of tools available for all applications running in your infrastructure.

Of course, with any technical choice, there are trade-offs between this modular container-based pattern and rolling your own code into your application. The library-based approach is always going to be somewhat less tailored to the specifics of your application. This means that it may be less efficient in terms of size of performance, or that the API may require some adaptation to fit into your environment. I would compare these trade-offs to the difference between buying off-the-rack clothing versus bespoke fashion. The bespoke fashion will always fit you better, but it will take longer to arrive and cost more to acquire. As with clothes, for most of us it makes sense to buy the more general-purpose solution when it comes to coding. Of course, if your application demands extremes in terms of performance, you can always choose the handwritten solution.

Hands On: Deploying the topz Container

To see the topz sidecar in action, you first need to deploy some other container to act as the application container. Choose an existing application that you are running and deploy it using Docker:

```
$ docker run -d <my-app-image>
<container-hash-value>
```

After you run that image, you will receive the identifier for that specific container. It will look something like: `cccf82b85000...` If you don't have it, you can always look it up using the `docker ps` command, which will show all currently running containers. Assuming you have stashed that value in an environment variable named `APP_ID`, you can then run the `topz` container in the same PID namespace using:

```
$ docker run --pid=container:${APP_ID} \
    -p 8080:8080 \
    brendanburns/topz:db0fa58 \
    /server --addr=0.0.0.0:8080
```

This will launch the `topz` sidecar in the same PID namespace as the application container. Note that you may need to change the port that the sidecar uses for serving if your application container is also running on port 8080. Once the sidecar is running, you can visit *http://localhost:8080/topz* to get a complete readout of the processes that are running in the application container and their resource usage.

You can mix this sidecar with any other existing container to easily get a view into how the container is using its resources via a web interface.

Building a Simple PaaS with Sidecars

The sidecar pattern can be used for more than adaptation and monitoring. It can also be used as a means to implement the complete logic for your application in a simplified, modular manner. As an example, imagine building a simple platform as a service (PaaS) built around the `git` workflow. Once you deploy this PaaS, simply pushing new code up to a Git repository results in that code being deployed to the running servers. We'll see how the sidecar pattern makes building this PaaS remarkably straightforward.

As previously stated, in the sidecar pattern there are two containers: the main application container and the sidecar. In our simple PaaS application, the main container is a Node.js server that implements a web server. The Node.js server is instrumented so that it automatically reloads the server when new files are updated. This is accomplished with the `nodemon` tool (*https://nodemon.io*).

The sidecar container shares a filesystem with the main application container and runs a simple loop that synchronizes the filesystem with an existing Git repository:

```
#!/bin/bash

while true; do
  git pull
  sleep 10
done
```

Obviously this script could be more complex, pulling from a specific branch instead of simply from HEAD. It is left purposefully simple to improve the readability of this example.

The Node.js application and Git synchronization sidecar are coscheduled and deployed together to implement our simple PaaS (Figure 2-4). Once deployed, every time new code is pushed to a Git repository, the code is automatically updated by the sidecar and reloaded by the server.

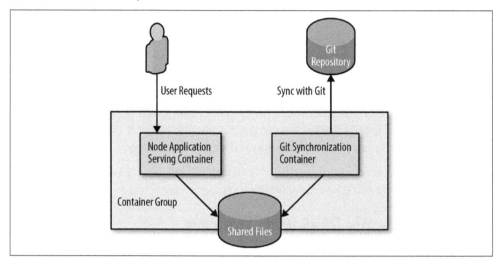

Figure 2-4. A simple sidecar-based PaaS

Designing Sidecars for Modularity and Reusability

In all of the examples of sidecars that we have detailed throughout this chapter, one of the most important themes is that every one was a modular, reusable artifact. To be successful, the sidecar should be reusable across a wide variety of applications and deployments. By achieving modular reuse, sidecars can dramatically speed up the building of your application.

However, this modularity and reusability, just like achieving modularity in high-quality software development requires focus and discipline. In particular, you need to focus on developing three areas:

- Parameterizing your containers
- Creating the API surface of your container
- Documenting the operation of your container

Parameterized Containers

Parameterizing your containers is the most important thing you can do to make your containers modular and reusable regardless of whether they are sidecars or not, though sidecars and other add-on containers are especially important to parameterize.

What do I mean when I say "parameterize"? Consider your container as a function in your program. How many parameters does it have? Each parameter represents an input that can customize a generic container to a specific situation. Consider, for example, the SSL add-on sidecar deployed previously. To be generally useful, it likely needs at least two parameters: the first is the name of the certificate being used to provide SSL, and the other is the port of the "legacy" application server running on localhost. Without these parameters, it is hard to imagine this sidecar container being usable for a broad array of applications. Similar parameters exist for all of the other sidecars described in this chapter.

Now that we know the parameters we want to expose, how do we actually expose them to users, and how do we consume them inside the container. There are two ways in which such parameters can be passed to your container: through environment variables or the command line. Though either is feasible, I have a general preference for passing parameters via environment variables. An example of passing such parameters to a sidecar container is:

```
docker run -e=PORT=<port> -d <image>
```

Of course, delivering values into the container is only part of the battle. The other part is actually using these variables inside the container. Typically, to do that, a simple shell script is used that loads the environment variables supplied with the sidecar container and either adjusts the configuration files or parameterizes the underlying application.

For example, you might pass in the certificate path and port as environment variables:

```
docker run -e=PROXY_PORT=8080 -e=CERTIFICATE_PATH=/path/to/cert.crt ...
```

In your container, you would use those variables to configure an `nginx.conf` file that points the web server to the correct file and proxy location.

Define Each Container's API

Given that you are parameterizing your containers, it is obvious that your containers are defining a "function" that is called whenever the container is executed. This function is clearly a part of the API that is defined by your container, but there are other parts to this API as well, including calls that the container will make to other services as well as traditional HTTP or other APIs that the container provides.

As you think about defining modular, reusable containers, it is important to realize that all aspects of how your container interacts with its world are part of the API defined by that reusable container. As in the world of microservices, these *micro-containers* rely on APIs to ensure that there is a clean separation between the main application container and the sidecar. Additionally the API exists to ensure that all consumers of the sidecar will continue to work correctly as subsequent versions are released. Likewise, having a clean API for a sidecar enables the sidecar developer to move more quickly since they have a clear definition (and hopefully unit tests) for the services they provide as a part of the sidecar.

To see a concrete example of why this API surface area is important, consider the configuration management sidecar we discussed earlier. A useful configuration for this sidecar might be UPDATE_FREQUENCY, which indicates how often the configuration should be synchronized with the filesystem. It is clear that if, at some later time, the name of the parameter is changed to UPDATE_PERIOD, this change would be a violation of the sidecar's API and clearly would break it for some users.

While that example is obvious, even more subtle changes can break the sidecar API. Imagine, for example, that UPDATE_FREQUENCY originally took a number in seconds. Over time and with feedback from users, the sidecar developer determined that specifying seconds for large time values (e.g., minutes) was annoying users and changed the parameter to accept strings (10 m, 5 s, etc.). Because old parameter values (e.g., 10, for 10 seconds) won't parse in this new scheme, this is a breaking API change. Suppose still that the developer anticipated this but made values without units parse to milliseconds where they had previously parsed to seconds. Even this change, despite not leading to an error, is a breaking API change for the sidecar since it will lead to significantly more frequent configuration checks and correspondingly more load on the cloud configuration server.

I hope this discussion has shown you that for true modularity, you need to be very conscious of the API that your sidecar provides, and that "breaking" changes to that API may not always be as obvious as changing the name of a parameter.

Documenting Your Containers

By now, you've seen how you can parameterize your sidecar containers to make them modular and reuseable. You've learned about the importance of maintaining a stable API to ensure that you don't break sidecars for your users. But there's one final step to building modular, reusable containers: ensuring that people can use them in the first place.

As with software libraries, the key to building something truly useful is explaining how to use it. There is little good in building a flexible, reliable modular container if no one can figure out how to use it. Sadly, there are few formal tools available for documenting container images, but there are some best practices you can use to accomplish this.

For every container image, the most obvious place to look for documentation is the `Dockerfile` from which the container was built. There are some parts of the `Docker file` that already document how the container works. One example of this is the `EXPOSE` directive, which indicates the ports that the image listens on. Even though `EXPOSE` is not necessary, it is a good practice to include it in your `Dockerfile` and also to add a comment that explains what exactly is listening on that port. For example:

```
...

# Main web server runs on port 8080
EXPOSE 8080
...
```

Additionally, if you use environment variables to parameterize your container, you can use the `ENV` directive to set default values for those parameters as well as document their usage:

```
...

# The PROXY_PORT parameter indicates the port on localhost to redirect
# traffic to.
ENV PROXY_PORT 8000
...
```

Finally, you should always use the `LABEL` directive to add metadata for your image; for example, the maintainer's email address, web page, and version of the image:

```
...

LABEL "org.label-schema.vendor"="name@company.com"
LABEL "org.label.url"="http://images.company.com/my-cool-image"
LABEL "org.label-schema.version"="1.0.3"
...
```

The names for these labels are drawn from the schema established by the Label Schema project (*http://label-schema.org/rc1*). The project is working to establish a shared set of well-known labels. By using a common taxonomy of image labels, multiple different tools can rely on the same meta information in order to visualize, monitor, and correctly use an application. By adopting shared terms, you can use the set of tools developed in the community without modifying your image. Of course, you can also add whatever additional labels make sense in the context of your image.

Summary

Over the course of this chapter, we've introduced the sidecar pattern for combining containers on a single machine. In the sidecar pattern, a sidecar container augments and extends an application container to add functionality. Sidecars can be used to update existing legacy applications when changing the application is too costly. Likewise, they can be used to create modular utility containers that standardize implementations of common functionality. These utility containers can be reused in a large number of applications, increasing consistency and reducing the cost of developing each application. Subsequent chapters introduce other single-node patterns that demonstrate other uses for modular, reusable containers.

## CHAPTER 3

Ambassadors

The previous chapter introduced the sidecar pattern, where one container augments a pre-existing container to add functionality. This chapter introduces the ambassador pattern, where an ambassador container brokers interactions between the application container and the rest of the world. As with other single-node patterns, the two containers are tightly linked in a symbiotic pairing that is scheduled to a single machine. A canonical diagram of this pattern is shown in Figure 3-1.

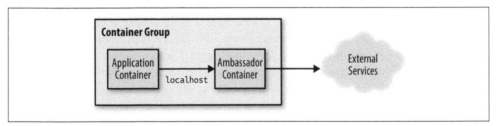

Figure 3-1. Generic ambassador pattern

The value of the ambassador pattern is twofold. First, as with the other single-node patterns, there is inherent value in building modular, reusable containers. The separation of concerns makes the containers easier to build and maintain. Likewise, the ambassador container can be reused with a number of different application containers. This reuse speeds up application development because the container's code can be reused in a number of places. Additionally the implementation is both more consistent and of a higher quality because it is built once and used in many different contexts.

The rest of this chapter provides a number of examples of using the ambassador pattern to implement a series of real-world applications.

Using an Ambassador to Shard a Service

Sometimes the data that you want to store in a storage layer becomes too big for a single machine to handle. In such situations, you need to *shard* your storage layer. Sharding splits up the layer into multiple disjoint pieces, each hosted by a separate machine. This chapter focuses on a single-node pattern for adapting an existing service to talk to a sharded service that exists somewhere in the world. It does not discuss how the sharded service came to exist. Sharding and a multi-node sharded service design pattern are discussed in great detail in Chapter 6. A diagram of a sharded service is shown in Figure 3-2.

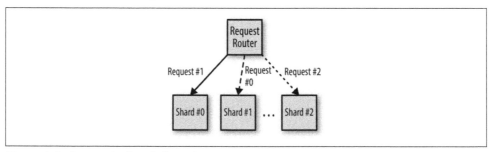

Figure 3-2. A generic sharded service

When deploying a sharded service, one question that arises is how to integrate it with the frontend or middleware code that stores data. Clearly there needs to be logic that routes a particular request to a particular shard, but often it is difficult to retrofit such a sharded client into existing source code that expects to connect to a single storage backend. Additionally, sharded services make it difficult to share configuration between development environments (where there is often only a single storage shard) and production environments (where there are often many storage shards).

One approach is to build all of the sharding logic into the sharded service itself. In this approach, the sharded service also has a stateless load balancer that directs traffic to the appropriate shard. Effectively, this load balancer is a distributed ambassador as a service. This makes a client-side ambassador unnecessary at the expense of a more complicated deployment for the sharded service. The alternative is to integrate a single-node ambassador on the client side to route traffic to the appropriate shard. This makes deploying the client somewhat more complicated but simplifies the deployment of the sharded service. As is always the case with trade-offs, it is up to the particulars of your specific application to determine which approach makes the most sense. Some factors to consider include where team lines fall in your architecture, as well as where you are writing code versus simply deploying off-the-shelf software. Ultimately, either choice is valid. The following section describes how to use the single-node ambassador pattern for client-side sharding.

When adapting an existing application to a sharded backend, you can introduce an ambassador container that contains all of the logic needed to route requests to the appropriate storage shard. Thus, your frontend or middleware application only connects to what appears to be a single storage backend running on localhost. However, this server is in fact actually a *sharding ambassador proxy*, which receives all of the requests from your application code, sends a request to the appropriate storage shard, and then returns the result to your application. This use of an ambassador is diagrammed in Figure 3-3.

The net result of applying the ambassador pattern to sharded services is a separation of concerns between the application container, which simply knows it needs to talk to a storage service and discovers that service on localhost, and the sharding ambassador proxy, which only contains the code necessary to perform appropriate sharding. As with all good single-node patterns, this ambassador can be reused between many different applications. Or, as we'll see in the following hands-on example, an off-the-shelf open source implementation can be used for the ambassador, speeding up the development of the overall distributed system.

Hands On: Implementing a Sharded Redis

Redis is a fast key-value store that can be used as a cache or for more persistent storage. In this example, we'll be using it as a cache. We'll begin by deploying a sharded Redis service to a Kubernetes cluster. We'll use the StatefulSet API object to deploy it, since it will give us unique DNS names for each shard that we can use when configuring the proxy.

The StatefulSet for Redis looks like this:

```
apiVersion: apps/v1beta1
kind: StatefulSet
metadata:
  name: sharded-redis
spec:
  serviceName: "redis"
  replicas: 3
  template:
    metadata:
      labels:
        app: redis
    spec:
      terminationGracePeriodSeconds: 10
      containers:
      - name: redis
        image: redis
        ports:
        - containerPort: 6379
          name: redis
```

Save this to a file named *redis-shards.yaml* and you can deploy this with `kubectl create -f redis-shards.yaml`. This will create three containers running redis. You can see these by running `kubectl get pods`; you should see `sharded-redis-[0,1,2]`.

Of course, just running the replicas isn't sufficient; we also need names by which we can refer to the replicas. In this case, we'll use a Kubernetes `Service`, which will create DNS names for the replicas we have created. The `Service` looks like this:

```
apiVersion: v1
kind: Service
metadata:
  name: redis
  labels:
    app: redis
spec:
  ports:
  - port: 6379
    name: redis
  clusterIP: None
  selector:
    app: redis
```

Save this to a file named *redis-service.yaml* and deploy with `kubectl create -f redis-service.yaml`. You should now have DNS entries for `sharded-redis-0.redis`, `sharded-redis-1.redis`, etc. We can use these names to configure `twemproxy`. `twemproxy` is a lightweight, highly performant proxy for `memcached` and Redis, which was originally developed by Twitter and is open source and available on GitHub (*https://github.com/twitter/twemproxy*). We can configure `twemproxy` to point to the replicas we created by using the following configuration:

```
redis:
  listen: 127.0.0.1:6379
  hash: fnv1a_64
  distribution: ketama
  auto_eject_hosts: true
  redis: true
  timeout: 400
  server_retry_timeout: 2000
  server_failure_limit: 1
  servers:
  - sharded-redis-0.redis:6379:1
  - sharded-redis-1.redis:6379:1
  - sharded-redis-2.redis:6379:1
```

In this config, you can see that we are serving the Redis protocol on `localhost:6379` so that the application container can access the ambassador. We will deploy this into our ambassador pod using a Kubernetes `ConfigMap` object that we can create with:

```
kubectl create configmap twem-config --from-file=./nutcracker.yaml
```

Finally, all of the preparations are done and we can deploy our ambasssador example. We define a pod that looks like:

```
apiVersion: v1
kind: Pod
metadata:
  name: ambassador-example
spec:
  containers:
    # This is where the application container would go, for example
    # - name: nginx
    #   image: nginx
    # This is the ambassador container
    - name: twemproxy
      image: ganomede/twemproxy
      command:
      - "nutcracker"
      - "-c"
      - "/etc/config/nutcracker.yaml"
      - "-v"
      - "7"
      - "-s"
      - "6222"
      volumeMounts:
      - name: config-volume
        mountPath: /etc/config
  volumes:
    - name: config-volume
      configMap:
        name: twem-config
```

This pod defines the ambassador; then the specific user's application container can be injected to complete the pod.

Using an Ambassador for Service Brokering

When trying to render an application portable across multiple environments (e.g., public cloud, physical datacenter, or private cloud), one of the primary challenges is service discovery and configuration. To understand what this means, imagine a frontend that relies on a MySQL database to store its data. In the public cloud, this MySQL service might be provided as software-as-a-service (SaaS), whereas in a private cloud it might be necessary to dynamically spin up a new virtual machine or container running MySQL.

Consequently, building a portable application requires that the application know how to introspect its environment and find the appropriate MySQL service to connect to. This process is called *service discovery*, and the system that performs this discovery and linking is commonly called a *service broker*. As with previous examples, the ambassador pattern enables a system to separate the logic of the application container from the logic of the service broker ambassador. The application simply always connects to an instance of the service (e.g., MySQL) running on localhost. It is the responsibility of the service broker ambassador to introspect its environment and broker the appropriate connection. This process is shown in Figure 3-3.

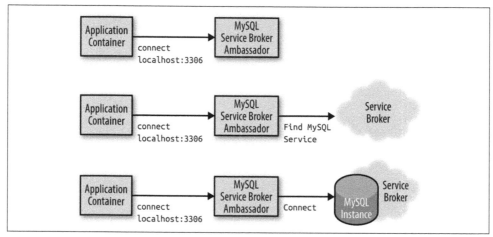

Figure 3-3. A service broker ambassador creating a MySQL service

Using an Ambassador to Do Experimentation or Request Splitting

A final example application of the ambassador pattern is to perform experimentation or other forms of request splitting. In many production systems, it is advantageous to be able to perform request splitting, where some fraction of all requests are not serviced by the main production service but rather are redirected to a different implementation of the service. Most often, this is used to perform experiments with new, beta versions of the service to determine if the new version of the software is reliable or comparable in performance to the currently deployed version.

Additionally, request splitting is sometimes used to `tee` or split traffic such that all traffic goes to both the production system as well as a newer, undeployed version. The responses from the production system are returned to the user, while the responses from the `tee`-d service are ignored. Most often, this form of request splitting is used to simulate production load on the new version of the service without risking impact to existing production users.

Given the previous examples, it is straightforward to see how a request-splitting ambassador can interact with an application container to implement request splitting. As before, the application container simply connects to the service on localhost, while the ambassador container receives the requests, proxies responses to both the production and experimental systems, and then returns the production responses back as if it had performed the work itself.

This separation of concerns keeps the code in each container slim and focused, and the modular factoring of the application ensures that the request-splitting ambassador can be reused for a variety of different applications and settings.

Hands On: Implementing 10% Experiments

To implement our request-splitting experiment, we're going to use the nginx web server. Nginx is a powerful, richly featured open source server. To configure nginx as the ambassador, we'll use the following configuration (note that this is for HTTP but it could easily be adapted for HTTPS as well).

```
worker_processes  5;
error_log  error.log;
pid        nginx.pid;
worker_rlimit_nofile 8192;

events {
  worker_connections  1024;
}

http {
    upstream backend {
        ip_hash;
        server web weight=9;
        server experiment;
    }

    server {
        listen localhost:80;
        location / {
            proxy_pass http://backend;
        }
    }
}
```

 As with the previous discussion of sharded services, it's also possible to deploy the experiment framework as a separate microservice in front of your application instead of integrating it as a part of your client pods. Of course, by doing this you are introducing another service that needs to be maintained, scaled, monitored, etc. If experimentation is likely to be a longstanding component in your architecture, this might be worthwhile. If it is used more occasionally, then a client-side ambassador might make more sense.

You'll note that I'm using IP hashing in this configuration. This is important because it ensures that the user doesn't flip-flop back and forth between the experiment and the main site. This assures that every user has a consistent experience with the application.

The `weight` parameter is used to send 90% of the traffic to the main existing application, while 10% of the traffic is redirected to the experiment.

As with other examples, we'll deploy this configuration as a `ConfigMap` object in Kubernetes:

```
kubectl create configmaps --from-file=nginx.conf
```

Of course, this assumes that you have both a `web` and `experiment` service defined. If you don't, you need to create them now before you try to create the ambassador container, since nginx doesn't like to start if it can't find the services it is proxying to. Here are some example service configs:

```
# This is the 'experiment' service
apiVersion: v1
kind: Service
metadata:
  name: experiment
  labels:
    app: experiment
spec:
  ports:
  - port: 80
    name: web
  selector:
    # Change this selector to match your application's labels
    app: experiment
---
# This is the 'prod' service
apiVersion: v1
kind: Service
metadata:
  name: web
  labels:
    app: web
spec:
  ports:
  - port: 80
    name: web
  selector:
    # Change this selector to match your application's labels
    app: web
```

And then we will deploy nginx itself as the ambassador container within a pod:

```
apiVersion: v1
kind: Pod
```

```yaml
metadata:
  name: experiment-example
spec:
  containers:
    # This is where the application container would go, for example
    # - name: some-name
    #   image: some-image
    # This is the ambassador container
    - name: nginx
      image: nginx
      volumeMounts:
      - name: config-volume
        mountPath: /etc/nginx
  volumes:
    - name: config-volume
      configMap:
        name: experiment-config
```

You can add a second (or third, or fourth) container to the pod to take advantage of the ambassador.

## CHAPTER 4

Adapters

In the preceding chapters, we saw how the sidecar pattern can extend and augment existing application containers. We also saw how ambassadors can alter and broker how an application container communicates with the external world. This chapter describes the final single-node pattern: the *adapter* pattern. In the adapter pattern, the *adapter container* is used to modify the interface of the *application container* so that it conforms to some predefined interface that is expected of all applications. For example, an adapter might ensure that an application implements a consistent monitoring interface. Or it might ensure that log files are always written to stdout or any number of other conventions.

Real-world application development is a heterogeneous, hybrid exercise. Some parts of your application might be written from scratch by your team, some supplied by vendors, and some might consist entirely of off-the-shelf open source or proprietary software that you consume as precompiled binary. The net effect of this heterogeneity is that any real-world application you deploy will have been written in a variety of languages, with a variety of conventions for logging, monitoring, and other common services.

Yet, to effectively monitor and operate your application, you need common interfaces. When each application provides metrics using a different format and interface, it is very difficult to collect all of those metrics in a single place for visualization and alerting. This is where the adapter pattern is relevant. Like other single-node patterns, the adapter pattern is made up of modular containers. Different application containers can present many different monitoring interfaces while the adapter container adapts this heterogeneity to present a consistent interface. This enables you to deploy a single tool that expects this single interface. Figure 4-1 illustrates this general pattern.

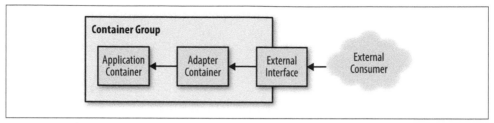

Figure 4-1. The generic adapter pattern

The remainder of this chapter gives several different applications of the adapter pattern.

Monitoring

When monitoring your software, you want a single solution that can automatically discover and monitor any application that is deployed into your environment. To make this feasible, every application has to implement the same monitoring interface. There are numerous examples of standardized monitoring interfaces, such as `syslog`, event tracing on Windows (etw), JMX for Java applications, and many, many other protocols and interfaces. However, each of these is unique in both protocol for communication as well as the style of communication (push versus pull).

Sadly, applications in your distributed system are likely to span the gamut from code that you have written yourself to off-the-shelf open source components. As a result, you will find yourself with a wide range of different monitoring interfaces that you need to integrate into a single well-understood system.

Fortunately, most monitoring solutions understand that they need to be widely applicable, and thus they have implemented a variety of plugins that can adapt one monitoring format to a common interface. Given this set of tools, how can we deploy and manage our applications in an agile and stable manner? Fortunately, the adapter pattern can provide us with the answers. Applying the adapter pattern to monitoring, we see that the application container is simply the application that we want to monitor. The adapter container contains the tools for transforming the monitoring interface exposed by the application container into the interface expected by the general-purpose monitoring system.

Decoupling the system in this fashion makes for a more comprehensible, maintainable system. Rolling out new versions of the application doesn't require a rollout of the monitoring adapter. Additionally, the monitoring container can be reused with multiple different application containers. The monitoring container may even have been supplied by the monitoring system maintainers independent of the application developers. Finally, deploying the monitoring adapter as a separate container ensures that each container gets its own dedicated resources in terms of both CPU and memory.

This ensures that a misbehaving monitoring adapter cannot cause problems with a user-facing service.

Hands On: Using Prometheus for Monitoring

As an example, consider monitoring your containers via the Prometheus open source project (*https://prometheus.io*). Prometheus is a monitoring aggregator, which collects metrics and aggregates them into a single time-series database. On top of this database, Prometheus provides visualization and query language for introspecting the collected metrics. To collect metrics from a variety of different systems, Prometheus expects every container to expose a specific `metrics` API. This enables Prometheus to monitor a wide variety of different programs through a single interface.

However, many popular programs, such as the Redis key-value store, do not export metrics in a format that is compatible with Prometheus. Consequently, the adapter pattern is quite useful for taking an existing service like Redis and adapting it to the Prometheus metrics-collection interface.

Consider a simple Kubernetes pod definition for a Redis server:

```
apiVersion: v1
kind: Pod
metadata:
  name: adapter-example
  namespace: default
spec:
  containers:
  - image: redis
    name: redis
```

At this point, this container is not capable of being monitored by Prometheus because it does not export the right interface. However, if we simply add an adapter container (in this case, an open source Prometheus exporter), we can modify this pod to export the correct interface and thus adapt it to fit Prometheus's expectations:

```
apiVersion: v1
kind: Pod
metadata:
  name: adapter-example
  namespace: default
spec:
  containers:
  - image: redis
    name: redis
  # Provide an adapter that implements the Prometheus interface
  - image: oliver006/redis_exporter
    name: adapter
```

This example illustrates not only the value of the adapter pattern for ensuring a consistent interface, but also the value of container patterns in general for modular container reuse. In this case, the example shown combines an existing Redis container with an existing Prometheus adapter. The net effect is a monitorable Redis server, with little work on our part to deploy it. In the absence of the adapter pattern, the same deployment would have required significantly more custom work and would have resulted in a much less operable solution, since any updates to either Redis or the adapter would have required work to apply the update.

Logging

Much like monitoring, there is a wide variety of heterogeneity in how systems log data to an output stream. Systems might divide their logs into different levels (such as debug, info, warning, and error) with each level going into a different file. Some might simply log to `stdout` and `stderr`. This is especially problematic in the world of containerized applications where there is a general expectation that your containers will log to `stdout`, because that is what is available via commands like `docker logs` or `kubectl logs`.

Adding further complexity, the information logged generally has structured information (e.g., the date/time of the log), but this information varies widely between different logging libraries (e.g., Java's built-in logging versus the `glog` package for Go).

Of course, when you are storing and querying the logs for your distributed system, you don't really care about these differences in logging format. You want to ensure that despite different structures for the data, every log ends up with the appropriate timestamp.

Fortunately, as with monitoring, the adapter pattern can help provide a modular, reusable design for both of these situations. While the application container may log to a file, the adapter container can redirect that file to `stdout`. Different application containers can log information in different formats, but the adapter container can transform that data into a single structured representation that can be consumed by your log aggregator. Again, the adapter is taking a heterogeneous world of applications and creating a homogenous world of common interfaces.

One question that often comes up when considering adapter patterns is: Why not simply modify the application container itself? If you are the developer responsible for the application container, then this might actually be a good solution. Adapting your code or your container to implement a consistent interface can work well. However, in many cases we are reusing a container produced by another party. In such cases, deriving a slightly modified image that we have to maintain (patch, rebase, etc.) is significantly more expensive than developing an adapter container that can run alongside the other party's image. Additionally, decoupling the adapter into its own container allows for the possibility of sharing and reuse, which isn't possible when you modify the application container.

Hands On: Normalizing Different Logging Formats with Fluentd

One common task for an adapter is to normalize log metrics into a standard set of events. Many different applications have different output formats, but you can use a standard logging tool deployed as an adapter to normalize them all to a consistent format. In this example, we will use the fluentd monitoring agent as well as some community-supported plugins to obtain logs from a variety of different sources.

fluentd (*https://fluentd.org*) is one of the more popular open source logging agents available. One of its major features is a rich set of community-supported plugins that enable a great deal of flexibility in monitoring a variety of applications.

The first application that we will monitor is Redis. Redis is a popular key-value store; one of the commands it offers is the SLOWLOG command. This command lists recent queries that exceeded a particular time interval. Such information is quite useful in debugging your application's performance. Unfortunately, SLOWLOG is only available as a command on the Redis server, which means that it is difficult to use retrospectively if a problem happens when someone isn't available to debug the server. To fix this limitation, we can use fluentd and the adapter pattern to add slow-query logging to Redis.

To do this, we use the adapter pattern with a redis container as the main application container, and the fluentd container as our adapter container. In this case, we will also use the fluent-plugin-redis-slowlog (*https://github.com/mominosin/fluent-plugin-redis-slowlog*) fluentd plugin to listen to the slow queries. We can configure this plugin using the following snippet:

```
<source>
  type redis_slowlog
  host localhost
  port 6379
```

```
    tag redis.slowlog
  </source>
```

Because we are using an adapter and the containers both share a network namespace, configuring the logging simply uses `localhost` and the default Redis port (6379). Given this application of the adapter pattern, logging will always be available whenever we want to debug slow Redis queries.

A similar exercise can be done to monitor logs from the Apache Storm (*https:// storm.apache.org*) system. Again, Storm provides data via a RESTful API, which is useful but has limitations if we are not currently monitoring the system when a problem occurs. Like Redis, we can use a `fluentd` adapter to transfor the Storm process into a time series of queryable logs. To do this, we deploy a `fluentd` adapter with the `fluent-plugin-storm` plugin enabled. We can configure this plugin with a `fluentd` config pointed at localhost (because again, we are running as a container group with a shared localhost); the config for the plugin looks like:

```
<source>
  type storm
  tag storm
  url http://localhost:8080
  window 600
  sys 0
</source>
```

Adding a Health Monitor

One last example of applying the adapter pattern is derived from monitoring the health of an application container. Consider the task of monitoring the health of an off-the-shelf database container. In this case, the container for the database is supplied by the database project, and we would rather not modify that container simply to add health checks. Of course, a container orchestrator will allow us to add simple health checks to ensure that the process is running and that it is listening on a particular port, but what if we want to add richer health checks that actually run queries against the database?

Container orchestration systems like Kubernetes enable us to use shell scripts as health checks as well. Given this capability, we can write a rich shell script that runs a number of different diagnostic queries against the database to determine its health. But where can we store such a script and how can we version it?

The answer to these problems should be easy to guess by now: we can use an adapter container. The database runs in the application container and shares a network interface with the adapter container. The adapter container is a simple container that only contains the shell script for determining the health of the database. This script can then be set up as the health check for the database container and can perform whatever rich health checks our application requires. If these checks ever fail, the database will be automatically restarted.

Hands On: Adding Rich Health Monitoring for MySQL

Suppose then that you want to add deep monitoring on a MySQL database where you actually run a query that was representative of your workload. In this case, one option would be to update the MySQL container to contain a health check that is specific to your application. However, this is generally an unattractive idea because it requires that you both modify some existing MySQL base image as well as update that image as new MySQL images are released.

Using the adapter pattern is a much more attractive approach to adding health checks to your database container. Instead of modifying the existing MySQL container, you can add an additional adapter container to the pre-existing MySQL container, which runs the appropriate query to test the database health. Given that this adapter container implements the expected HTTP health check, it is simply a case of defining the MySQL database process's health check in terms of the interface exposed by this database adapter.

The source code for this adapter is relatively straightforward and looks like this in Go (though clearly other language implementations are possible as well):

```go
package main

import (
        "database/sql"
        "flag"
        "fmt"
        "net/http"

        _ "github.com/go-sql-driver/mysql"
)

var (
        user   = flag.String("user", "", "The database user name")
        passwd = flag.String("password", "", "The database password")
        db     = flag.String("database", "", "The database to connect to")
        query  = flag.String("query", "", "The test query")
        addr   = flag.String("address", "localhost:8080",
                            "The address to listen on")
)

// Basic usage:
//   db-check --query="SELECT * from my-cool-table" \
//            --user=bdburns \
//            --passwd="you wish"
//
func main() {
```

```
        flag.Parse()
        db, err := sql.Open("localhost",
                           fmt.Sprintf("%s:%s@/%s", *user, *passwd, *db))
        if err != nil {
                fmt.Printf("Error opening database: %v", err)
        }

    // Simple web handler that runs the query
        http.HandleFunc("", func(res http.ResponseWriter, req *http.Request) {
                _, err := db.Exec(*query)
                if err != nil {
                        res.WriteHeader(http.StatusInternalServerError)
                        res.Write([]byte(err.Error()))
                        return
                }
                res.WriteHeader(http.StatusOK)
                res.Write([]byte("OK"))
                return
        })
    // Startup the server
        http.ListenAndServe(*addr, nil)
}
```

We can then build this into a container image and pull it into a pod that looks like:

```
apiVersion: v1
kind: Pod
metadata:
  name: adapter-example-health
  namespace: default
spec:
  containers:
  - image: mysql
    name: mysql
  - image: brendanburns/mysql-adapter
    name: adapter
```

That way, the mysql container is unchanged, but the desired feedback about the health of the mysql server can still be obtained from the adapter container.

When looking at this application of the adapter pattern, it may seem like applying the pattern is superfluous. Clearly we could have built our own custom image that knew how to health check the mysql instance itself.

While this is true, this method ignores the strong benefits that derive from modularity. If every developer implements their own specific container with health checking built in, there are no opportunities for reuse or sharing.

In contrast, if we use patterns like the adapter to develop modular solutions comprised of multiple containers, the work is inherently decoupled and more easily shared. An adapter that is developed to health check mysql is a module that can be shared and reused by a variety of people. Further, people can apply the adapter pattern using this shared health-checking container, without having deep knowledge of how to health check a `mysql` database. Thus the modularity and adapter pattern serve not to just facilitate sharing, but also to empower people to take advantage of the knowledge of others.

Sometimes design patterns aren't just for the developers who apply them, but lead to the development of communities that can collaborate and share solutions between members of the community as well as the broader developer ecosystem.

## PART II

Serving Patterns

The previous chapter described patterns for grouping collections of containers that are scheduled on the same machine. These groups are tightly coupled, symbiotic systems. They depend on local, shared resources like disk, network interface, or inter-process communications. Such collections of containers are important patterns, but they are also building blocks for larger systems. Reliability, scalability, and separation of concerns dictate that real-world systems are built out of many different components, spread across multiple machines. In contrast to single-node patterns, the multi-node distributed patterns are more loosely coupled. While the patterns dictate patterns of communication between the components, this communication is based on network calls. Furthermore, many calls are issued in parallel, and systems coordinate via loose synchronization rather than tight constraints.

Introduction to Microservices

Recently, the term *microservices* has become a buzzword for describing multi-node distributed software architectures. Microservices describe a system built out of many different components running in different processes and communicating over defined APIs. Microservices stand in contrast to *monolithic* systems, which tend to place all of the functionality for a service within a single, tightly coordinated application. These two different architectural approaches are shown in Figures II-1 and II-2.

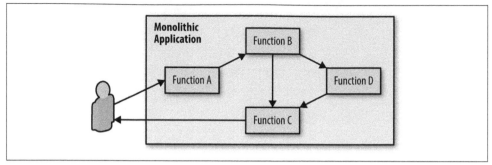

Figure II-1. A monolithic service with all functions in a single container

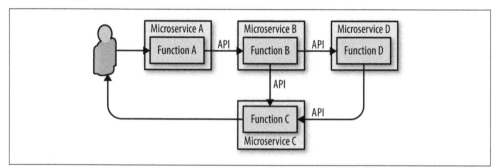

Figure II-2. A microservice architecture with each function broken out as a separate microservice

There are numerous benefits to the microservices approach, most of them are centered around reliability and agility. Microservices break down an application into small pieces, each focused on providing a single service. This reduced scope enables each service to be built and maintained by a single "two pizza" team. Reduced team size also reduces the overhead associated with keeping a team focused and moving in one direction.

Additionally, the introduction of formal APIs in between different microservices decouples the teams from one another and provides a reliable contract between the different services. This formal contract reduces the need for tight synchronization among the teams because the team providing the API understands the surface area that it needs to keep stable, and the team consuming the API can rely on a stable service without worrying about its details. This decoupling enables teams to independently manage their code and release schedules, which in turn improves each team's ability to iterate and improve their code.

Finally, the decoupling of microservices enables better scaling. Because each component has been broken out into its own service, it can be scaled independently. It is rare for each service within a larger application to grow at the same rate, or have the same way of scaling. Some systems are stateless and can simply scale horizontally, whereas other systems maintain state and require sharding or other approaches to scale. By separating each service out, each service can use the approach to scaling that suits it best. This is not possible when all services are part of a single monolith.

But of course there are downsides to the microservices approach to system design as well. The two foremost disadvantages are that because the system has become more loosely coupled, debugging the system when failures occur is significantly more difficult. You can no longer simply load a single application into a debugger and determine what went wrong. Any errors are the byproducts of a large number of systems often running on different machines. This environment is quite challenging to reproduce in a debugger. As a corollary, microservices-based systems are also difficult to design and architect. A microservices-based system uses multiple methods of communicating between services; different patterns (e.g., synchronous, asynchronous, message-passing, etc.); and multiple different patterns of coordination and control among the services.

These challenges are the motivation for distributed patterns. If a microservices architecture is made up of well-known patterns, then it is easier to design because many of the design practices are specified by the patterns. Additionally, patterns make the systems easier to debug because they enable developers to apply lessons learned across a number of different systems that use the same patterns.

With that in mind, this section introduces a number of multi-node patterns for building distributed systems. These patterns are not mutually exclusive. Any real-world system will be built from a collection of these patterns working together to produce a single higher-level application.

## CHAPTER 5

Replicated Load-Balanced Services

The simplest distributed pattern, and one that most are familiar with, is a replicated load-balanced service. In such a service, every server is identical to every other server and all are capable of supporting traffic. The pattern consists of a scalable number of servers with a load balancer in front of them. The load balancer is typically either completely round-robin or uses some form of session stickiness. The chapter will give a concrete example of how to deploy such a service in Kubernetes.

Stateless Services

Stateless services are ones that don't require saved state to operate correctly. In the simplest stateless applications, even individual requests may be routed to separate instances of the service (see Figure 5-1). Examples of stateless services include things like static content servers and complex middleware systems that receive and aggregate responses from numerous different backend systems.

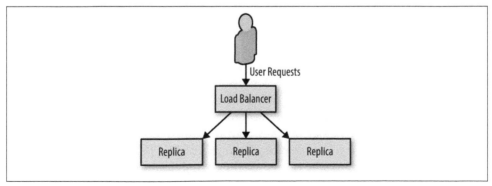

Figure 5-1. Basic replicated stateless service

Stateless systems are replicated to provide redundancy and scale. No matter how small your service is, you need at least two replicas to provide a service with a "highly available" service level agreement (SLA). To understand why this is true, consider trying to deliver a three-nines (99.9% availability). In a *three-nines service*, you get 1.4 minutes of downtime per day (24 × 60 × 0.001). Assuming that you have a service that never crashes, that still means you need to be able to do a software upgrade in less than 1.4 minutes in order to hit your SLA with a single instance. And that's assuming that you do daily software rollouts. If your team is really embracing continuous delivery and you're pushing a new version of software every hour, you need to be able to do a software rollout in 3.6 *seconds* to achieve your 99.9% uptime SLA with a single instance. Any longer than that and you will have more than 0.01% downtime from those 3.6 seconds.

Of course, instead of all of that work, you could just have two replicas of your service with a load balancer in front of them. That way, while you are doing a rollout, or in the—unlikely, I'm sure—event that your software crashes, your users will be served by the other replica of the service and never know anything was going on.

As services grow larger, they are also replicated to support additional users. *Horizontally scalable* systems handle more and more users by adding more replicas; see Figure 5-2. They achieve this with the load-balanced replicated serving pattern.

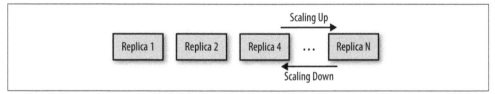

Figure 5-2. Horizontal scaling of a replicated stateless application

Readiness Probes for Load Balancing

Of course, simply replicating your service and adding a load balancer is only part of a complete pattern for stateless replicated serving. When designing a replicated service, it is equally important to build and deploy a readiness probe to inform the load balancer. We have discussed how health probes can be used by a container orchestration system to determine when an application needs to be restarted. In contrast, a *readiness probe* determines when an application is ready to serve user requests. The reason for the differentiation is that many applications require some time to become initialized before they are ready to serve. They may need to connect to databases, load plugins, or download serving files from the network. In all of these cases, the containers are *alive*, but they are not *ready*. When building an application for a replicated service pattern, be sure to include a special URL that implements this readiness check.

Hands On: Creating a Replicated Service in Kubernetes

The instructions below give a concrete example of how to deploy a stateless, replicated service behind a load balancer. These directions use the Kubernetes container orchestrator, but the pattern can be implemented on top of a number of different container orchestrators.

To begin with, we will create a small NodeJS application that serves definitions of words from the dictionary.

To try this service out, you can run it using a container image:

```
docker run -p 8080:8080 brendanburns/dictionary-server
```

This runs a simple dictionary server on your local machine. For example, you can visit *http://localhost:8080/dog* to see the definition for *dog*.

If you look at the logs for the container, you'll see that it starts serving immediately but only reports readiness after the dictionary (which is approximately 8 MB) has been downloaded over the network.

To deploy this in Kubernetes, you create a `Deployment`:

```yaml
apiVersion: extensions/v1beta1
kind: Deployment
metadata:
  name: dictionary-server
spec:
  replicas: 3
  template:
    metadata:
      labels:
        app: dictionary-server
    spec:
      containers:
      - name: server
        image: brendanburns/dictionary-server
        ports:
        - containerPort: 8080
        readinessProbe:
          httpGet:
            path: /ready
            port: 8080
          initialDelaySeconds: 5
          periodSeconds: 5
```

You can create this replicated, stateless service with:

```
kubectl create -f dictionary-deploy.yaml
```

Now that you have a number of replicas, you need a load balancer to bring requests to your replicas. The load balancer serves to distribute the load as well as to provide an abstraction to separate the replicated service from the consumers of the service. The load balancer also provides a resolvable name that is independent of any of the specific replicas.

With Kubernetes, you can create this load balancer with a `Service` object:

```
kind: Service
apiVersion: v1
metadata:
  name: dictionary-server-service
spec:
  selector:
    app: dictionary-server
  ports:
    - protocol: TCP
      port: 8080
      targetPort: 8080
```

Once you have the configuration file, you can create the dictionary service with:

```
kubectl create -f dictionary-service.yaml
```

Session Tracked Services

The previous examples of the stateless replicated pattern routed requests from all users to all replicas of a service. While this ensures an even distribution of load and fault tolerance, it is not always the preferred solution. Often there are reasons for wanting to ensure that a particular user's requests always end up on the same machine. Sometimes this is because you are caching that user's data in memory, so landing on the same machine ensures a higher cache hit rate. Sometimes it is because the interaction is long-running in nature, so some amount of state is maintained between requests. Regardless of the reason, an adaption of the stateless replicated service pattern is to use session tracked services, which ensure that all requests for a single user map to the same replica, as illustrated in Figure 5-3.

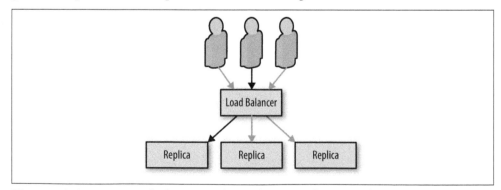

Figure 5-3. A session tracked service where all requests for a specific user are routed to a single instance

Generally speaking, this session tracking is performed by hashing the source and destination IP addresses and using that key to identify the server that should service the requests. So long as the source and destination IP addresses remain constant, all requests are sent to the same replica.

 IP-based session tracking works within a cluster (internal IPs) but generally doesn't work well with external IP addresses because of network address translation (NAT). For external session tracking, application-level tracking (e.g., via cookies) is preferred.

Often, session tracking is accomplished via a *consistent hashing function*. The benefit of a consistent hashing function becomes evident when the service is scaled up or down. Obviously, when the number of replicas changes, the mapping of a particular user to a replica may change. Consistent hashing functions minimize the number of users that actually change which replica they are mapped to, reducing the impact of scaling on your application.

Application-Layer Replicated Services

In all of the preceding examples, the replication and load balancing takes place in the network layer of the service. The load balancing is independent of the actual protocol that is being spoken over the network, beyond TCP/IP. However, many applications use HTTP as the protocol for speaking with each other, and knowledge of the application protocol that is being spoken enables further refinements to the replicated stateless serving pattern for additional functionality.

Introducing a Caching Layer

Sometimes the code in your stateless service is still expensive despite being stateless. It might make queries to a database to service requests or do a significant amount of rendering or data mixing to service the request. In such a world, a caching layer can make a great deal of sense. A cache exists between your stateless application and the end-user request. The simplest form of caching for web applications is a caching web proxy. The caching proxy is simply an HTTP server that maintains user requests in memory state. If two users request the same web page, only one request will go to your backend; the other will be serviced out of memory in the cache. This is illustrated in Figure 5-4.

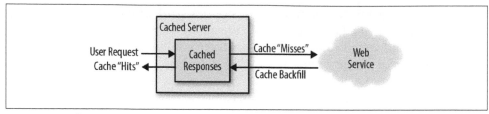

Figure 5-4. The operation of a cache server

For our purposes, we will use Varnish (*https://varnish-cache.org/*), an open source web cache.

Deploying Your Cache

The simplest way to deploy the web cache is alongside each instance of your web server using the sidecar pattern (see Figure 5-5).

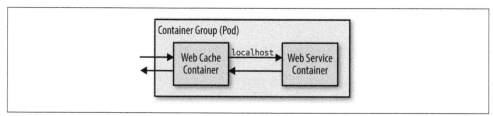

Figure 5-5. Adding the web cache server as a sidecar

Though this approach is simple, it has some disadvantages, namely that you will have to scale your cache at the same scale as your web servers. This is often not the approach you want. For your cache, you want as few replicas as possible with lots of resources for each replica (e.g., rather than 10 replicas with 1 GB of RAM each, you'd want two replicas with 5 GB of RAM each). To understand why this is preferable, consider that every page will be stored in every replica. With 10 replicas, you will store every page 10 times, reducing the overall set of pages that you can keep in memory in the cache. This causes a reduction in the *hit rate*, the fraction of the time that a request can be served out of cache, which in turn decreases the utility of the cache. Though you do want a few large caches, you might also want lots of small replicas of your web servers. Many languages (e.g., NodeJS) can really only utilize a single core, and thus you want many replicas to be able to take advantages of multiple cores, even on the same machine. Therefore, it makes the most sense to configure your caching layer as a second stateless replicated serving tier above your web-serving tier, as illustrated in Figure 5-6.

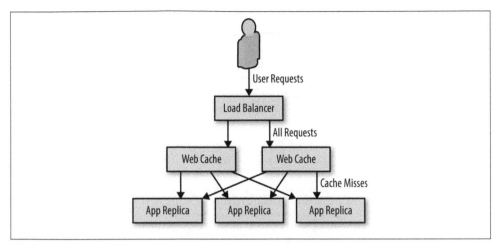

Figure 5-6. Adding the caching layer to our replicated service

 Unless you are careful, caching can break session tracking. The reason for this is that if you use default IP address affinity and load balancing, all requests will be sent from the IP addresses of the cache, not the end user of your service. If you've followed the advice previously given and deployed a few large caches, your IP-address-based affinity may in fact mean that some replicas of your web layer see *no* traffic. Instead, you need to use something like a cookie or HTTP header for session tracking.

Hands On: Deploying the Caching Layer

The dictionary-server service we built earlier distributes traffic to the dictionary server and is discoverable as the DNS name `dictionary-server-service`. This pattern is illustrated in Figure 5-7.

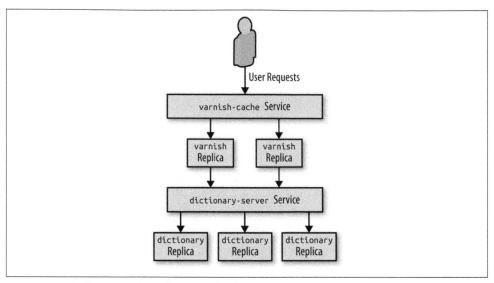

Figure 5-7. Adding a caching layer to the dictionary server

We can begin building this with the following Varnish cache configuration:

```
vcl 4.0;
backend default {
  .host = "dictionary-server-service";
  .port = "8080";
}
```

Create a `ConfigMap` object to hold this configuration:

```
kubectl create configmap varnish-config --from-file=default.vcl
```

Now we can deploy the replicated Varnish cache, which will load this configuration:

```
apiVersion: extensions/v1beta1
kind: Deployment
metadata:
  name: varnish-cache
spec:
  replicas: 2
  template:
    metadata:
      labels:
        app: varnish-cache
    spec:
      containers:
      - name: cache
        resources:
          requests:
            # We'll use two gigabytes for each varnish cache
            memory: 2Gi
```

```
    image: brendanburns/varnish
    command:
    - varnishd
    - -F
    - -f
    - /etc/varnish-config/default.vcl
    - -a
    - 0.0.0.0:8080
    - -s
    # This memory allocation should match the memory request above
    - malloc,2G
    ports:
    - containerPort: 8080
    volumeMounts:
    - name: varnish
      mountPath: /etc/varnish-config
  volumes:
  - name: varnish
    configMap:
      name: varnish-config
```

You can deploy the replicated Varnish servers with:

```
kubectl create -f varnish-deploy.yaml
```

And then finally deploy a load balancer for this Varnish cache:

```
kind: Service
apiVersion: v1
metadata:
  name: varnish-service
spec:
  selector:
    app: varnish-cache
  ports:
    - protocol: TCP
      port: 80
      targetPort: 8080
```

which you can create with:

```
kubectl create -f varnish-service.yaml
```

Expanding the Caching Layer

Now that we have inserted a caching layer into our stateless, replicated service, let's look at what this layer can provide beyond standard caching. HTTP reverse proxies like Varnish are generally pluggable and can provide a number of advanced features that are useful beyond caching.

Rate Limiting and Denial-of-Service Defense

Few of us build sites with the expectation that we will encounter a denial-of-service attack. But as more and more of us build APIs, a denial of service can come simply from a developer misconfiguring a client or a site-reliability engineer accidentally running a load test against a production installation. Thus, it makes sense to add general denial-of-service defense via rate limiting to the caching layer. Most HTTP reverse proxies like Varnish have capabilities along this line. In particular, Varnish has a `throttle` module that can be configured to provide throttling based on IP address and request path, as well as whether or not a user is logged in.

If you are deploying an API, it is generally a best practice to have a relatively small rate limit for anonymous access and then force users to log in to obtain a higher rate limit. Requiring a login provides auditing to determine who is responsible for the unexpected load, and also offers a barrier to would-be attackers who need to obtain multiple identities to launch a successful attack.

When a user hits the rate limit, the server will return the `429` error code indicating that too many requests have been issued. However, many users want to understand how many requests they have left before hitting that limit. To that end, you will likely also want to populate an HTTP header with the remaining-calls information. Though there isn't a standard header for returning this data, many APIs return some variation of `X-RateLimit-Remaining`.

SSL Termination

In addition to performing caching for performance, one of the other common tasks performed by the edge layer is SSL termination. Even if you plan on using SSL for communication between layers in your cluster, you should still use different certificates for the edge and your internal services. Indeed, each individual internal service should use its own certificate to ensure that each layer can be rolled out independently. Unfortunately, the Varnish web cache can't be used for SSL termination, but fortunately, the `nginx` application can. Thus we want to add a third layer to our stateless application pattern, which will be a replicated layer of `nginx` servers that will handle SSL termination for HTTPS traffic and forward traffic on to our Varnish cache. HTTP traffic continues to travel to the Varnish web cache, and Varnish forwards traffic on to our web application, as shown in Figure 5-8.

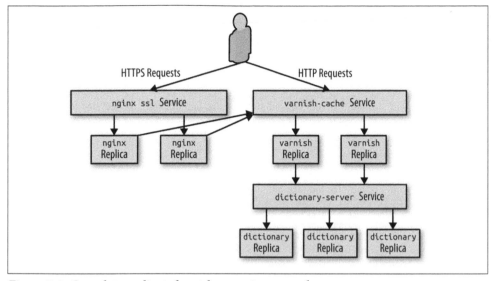

Figure 5-8. Complete replicated stateless serving example

Hands On: Deploying nginx and SSL Termination

The following instructions describe how to add a replicated SSL terminating nginx to the replicated service and cache that we previously deployed.

These instructions assume that you have a certificate. If you need to obtain a certificate, the easiest way to do that is via the tools at Let's Encrypt (*https://letsencrypt.org*). Alternately, you can use the `openssl` tool to create them. The following instructions assume that you've named them `server.crt` (public certificate) and `server.key` (private key on the server). Such self-signed certificates will cause security alerts in modern web browsers and should never be used for production.

The first step is to upload your certificate as a secret to Kubernetes:

```
kubectl create secret tls ssl --cert=server.crt --key=server.key
```

Once you have uploaded your certificate as a secret you need to create an nginx configuration to serve SSL:

```
events {
  worker_connections  1024;
}

http {
  server {
    listen 443 ssl;
```

```
    server_name my-domain.com www.my-domain.com;
    ssl on;
    ssl_certificate           /etc/certs/tls.crt;
    ssl_certificate_key       /etc/certs/tls.key;
    location / {
        proxy_pass http://varnish-service:80;
        proxy_set_header Host $host;
        proxy_set_header X-Forwarded-For $proxy_add_x_forwarded_for;
        proxy_set_header X-Forwarded-Proto $scheme;
        proxy_set_header X-Real-IP $remote_addr;
    }
  }
}
```

As with Varnish, you need to transform this into a `ConfigMap` object:

```
kubectl create configmap nginx-conf --from-file=nginx.conf
```

Now that you have a secret and an nginx configuration, it is time to create the replicated, stateless nginx layer:

```
apiVersion: extensions/v1beta1
kind: Deployment
metadata:
  name: nginx-ssl
spec:
  replicas: 4
  template:
    metadata:
      labels:
        app: nginx-ssl
    spec:
      containers:
      - name: nginx
        image: nginx
        ports:
        - containerPort: 443
        volumeMounts:
        - name: conf
          mountPath: /etc/nginx
        - name: certs
          mountPath: /etc/certs
      volumes:
      - name: conf
        configMap:
          # This is the ConfigMap for nginx we created previously
          name: nginx-conf
      - name: certs
        secret:
          # This is the secret we created above
          secretName: ssl
```

To create the replicated nginx servers, you use:

```
kubectl create -f nginx-deploy.yaml
```

Finally, you can expose this nginx SSL server with a service:

```
kind: Service
apiVersion: v1
metadata:
  name: nginx-service
spec:
  selector:
    app: nginx-ssl
  type: LoadBalancer
  ports:
    - protocol: TCP
      port: 443
      targetPort: 443
```

To create this load-balancing service run:

```
kubectl create -f nginx-service.yaml
```

If you create this service on a Kubernetes cluster that supports external load balancers, this will create an externalized, public service that services traffic on a public IP address.

To get this IP address, you can run:

```
kubectl get services
```

You should then be able to access the service with your web browser.

Summary

This chapter began with a simple pattern for replicated stateless services. Then we saw how this pattern grows with two additional replicated load-balanced layers to provide caching for performance, and SSL termination for secure web serving. This complete pattern for stateless replicated serving is shown in Figure 5-8.

This complete pattern can be deployed into Kubernetes using three `Deployments` and `Service` load balancers to connect the layers shown in Figure 5-8. The complete source for these examples can be found at *https://github.com/brendandburns/designing-distributed-systems*.

## CHAPTER 6

Sharded Services

In the previous chapter, we saw the value of replicating stateless services for reliability, redundancy, and scaling. This chapter considers sharded services. With the replicated services that we introduced in the preceding chapter, each replica was entirely homogeneous and capable of serving every request. In contrast to replicated services, with sharded services, each replica, or *shard*, is only capable of serving a subset of all requests. A load-balancing node, or *root*, is responsible for examining each request and distributing each request to the appropriate shard or shards for processing. The contrast between replicated and sharded services is represented in Figure 6-1.

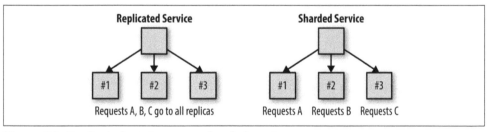

Figure 6-1. Replicated service versus sharded service

Replicated services are generally used for building stateless services, whereas sharded services are generally used for building stateful services. The primary reason for sharding the data is because the size of the state is too large to be served by a single machine. Sharding enables you to scale a service in response to the size of the state that needs to be served.

Sharded Caching

To completely illustrate the design of a sharded system, this section provides a deep dive into the design of a sharded caching system. A *sharded cache* is a cache that sits between the user requests and the actually frontend implementation. A high-level diagram of the system is shown in Figure 6-2.

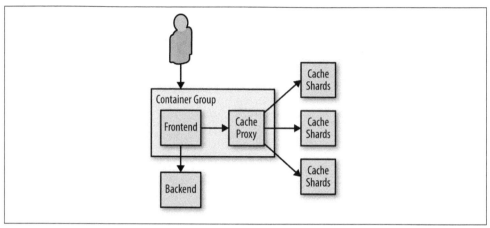

Figure 6-2. A sharded cache

In Chapter 3, we discussed how an ambassador could be used to distribute data to a sharded service. This section discusses how to build that service. When designing a sharded cache, there are a number of design aspects to consider:

- Why you might need a sharded cache
- The role of the cache in your architecture
- Replicated, sharded caches
- The sharding function

Why You Might Need a Sharded Cache

As was mentioned in the introduction, the primary reason for sharding any service is to increase the size of the data being stored in the service. To understand how this helps a caching system, imagine the following system: Each cache has 10 GB of RAM available to store results, and can serve 100 requests per second (RPS). Suppose then that our service has a total of 200 GB possible results that could be returned, and an expected 1,000 RPS. Clearly, we need 10 replicas of the cache in order to satisfy 1,000 RPS (10 replicas × 100 requests per second per replica). The simplest way to deploy this service would be as a replicated service, as described in the previous chapter. But deployed this way, the distributed cache can only hold a maximum of 5% (10 GB/200 GB) of the total data set that we are serving. This is because each cache replica is independent, and thus each cache replica stores roughly the exact same data in the cache. This is great for redundancy, but pretty terrible for maximizing memory utilization. If instead, we deploy a 10-way sharded cache, we can still serve the appropriate number of RPS (10 × 100 is still 1,000), but because each cache serves a completely unique set of data, we are able to store 50% (10 × 10 GB/200 GB) of the total data set. This tenfold increase in cache storage means that the memory for the cache is much better utilized, since each key exists only in a single cache.

The Role of the Cache in System Performance

In Chapter 5 we discussed how caches can be used to optimize end-user performance and latency, but one thing that wasn't covered was the criticality of the cache to your application's performance, reliability, and stability.

Put simply, the important question for you to consider is: If the cache were to fail, what would the impact be for your users and your service?

When we discussed the replicated cache, this question was less relevant because the cache itself was horizontally scalable, and failures of specific replicas would only lead to transient failures. Likewise, the cache could be horizontally scaled in response to increased load without impacting the end user.

This changes when you consider sharded caches. Because a specific user or request is always mapped to the same shard, if that shard fails, that user or request will always miss the cache until the shard is restored. Given the nature of a cache as transient data, this miss is not inherently a problem, and your system must know how to recalculate the data. However, this recalculation is inherently slower than using the cache directly, and thus it has performance implications for your end users.

The performance of your cache is defined in terms of its *hit rate*. The hit rate is the percentage of the time that your cache contains the data for a user request. Ultimately, the hit rate determines the overall capacity of your distributed system and affects the overall capacity and performance of your system.

Imagine, if you will, that you have a request-serving layer that can handle 1,000 RPS. After 1,000 RPS, the system starts to return HTTP 500 errors to users. If you place a cache with a 50% hit rate in front of this request-serving layer, adding this cache increases your maximum RPS from 1,000 RPS to 2,000 RPS. To understand why this is true, you can see that of the 2,000 inbound requests, 1,000 (50%) can be serviced by the cache, leaving 1,000 requests to be serviced by your serving layer. In this instance, the cache is fairly critical to your service, because if the cache fails, then the serving layer will be overloaded and half of all your user requests will fail. Given this, it likely makes sense to rate your service at a maximum of 1,500 RPS rather than the full 2,000 RPS. If you do this, then you can sustain a failure of half of your cache replicas and still keep your service stable.

But the performance of your system isn't just defined in terms of the number of requests that it can process. Your system's end-user performance is defined in terms of the *latency* of requests as well. A result from a cache is generally significantly faster than calculating that result from scratch. Consequently, a cache can improve the speed of requests as well as the total number of requests processed. To see why this is true, imagine that your system can serve a request from a user in 100 milliseconds. You add a cache with a 25% hit rate that can return a result in 10 milliseconds. Thus, the average latency for a request in your system is now 77.5 milliseconds. Unlike maximum requests per second, the cache simply makes your requests faster, so there is somewhat less need to worry about the fact that requests will slow down if the cache fails or is being upgraded. However, in some cases, the performance impact can cause too many user requests to pile up in request queues and ultimately time out. It's always recommended that you load test your system both with and without caches to understand the impact of the cache on the overall performance of your system.

Finally, it isn't just failures that you need to think about. If you need to upgrade or redeploy a sharded cache, you can not just deploy a new replica and assume it will take the load. Deploying a new version of a sharded cache will generally result in temporarily losing some capacity. Another, more advanced option is to replicate your shards.

Replicated, Sharded Caches

Sometimes your system is so dependent on a cache for latency or load that it is not acceptable to lose an entire cache shard if there is a failure or you are doing a rollout. Alternatively, you may have so much load on a particular cache shard that you need to scale it to handle the load. For these reasons, you may choose to deploy a sharded, replicated service. A sharded, replicated service combines the replicated service pattern described in the previous chapter with the sharded pattern described in previous sections. In a nutshell, rather than having a single server implement each shard in the cache, a replicated service is used to implement each cache shard.

This design is obviously more complicated to implement and deploy, but it has several advantages over a simple sharded service. Most importantly, by replacing a single server with a replicated service, each cache shard is resilient to failures and is always present during failures. Rather than designing your system to be tolerant to performance degradation resulting from cache shard failures, you can rely on the performance improvements that the cache provides. Assuming that you are willing to over-provision shard capacity, this means that it is safe for you to do a cache rollout during peak traffic, rather than waiting for a quiet period for your service.

Additionally, because each replicated cache shard is an independent replicated service, you can scale each cache shard in response to its load; this sort of "hot sharding" is discussed at the end of this chapter.

Hands On: Deploying an Ambassador and Memcache for a Sharded Cache

In Chapter 3 we saw how to deploy a sharded Redis service. Deploying a sharded memcache is similar.

First, we will deploy memcache as a Kubernetes `StatefulSet`:

```
apiVersion: apps/v1beta1
kind: StatefulSet
metadata:
  name: sharded-memcache
spec:
  serviceName: "memcache"
  replicas: 3
  template:
    metadata:
      labels:
        app: memcache
    spec:
      terminationGracePeriodSeconds: 10
      containers:
      - name: memcache
        image: memcached
        ports:
        - containerPort: 11211
          name: memcache
```

Save this to a file named *memcached-shards.yaml* and you can deploy this with `kubectl create -f memcached-shards.yaml`. This will create three containers running memcached.

As with the sharded Redis example, we also need to create a Kubernetes `Service` that will create DNS names for the replicas we have created. The service looks like this:

```
apiVersion: v1
kind: Service
metadata:
  name: memcache
  labels:
    app: memcache
spec:
  ports:
  - port: 11211
    name: memcache
  clusterIP: None
  selector:
    app: memcache
```

Save this to a file named *memcached-service.yaml* and deploy it with `kubectl create -f memcached-service.yaml`. You should now have DNS entries for memcache-0.memcache, memcache-1.memcache, etc. As with Redis, we can use these names to configure twemproxy (*https://github.com/twitter/twemproxy*).

```
memcache:
  listen: 127.0.0.1:11211
  hash: fnv1a_64
  distribution: ketama
  auto_eject_hosts: true
  timeout: 400
  server_retry_timeout: 2000
  server_failure_limit: 1
  servers:
   - memcache-0.memcache:11211:1
   - memcache-1.memcache:11211:1
   - memcache-2.memcache:11211:1
```

In this config, you can see that we are serving the memcache protocol on `localhost:11211` so that the application container can access the ambassador. We will deploy this into our ambassador pod using a Kubernetes `ConfigMap` object that we can create with: `kubectl create configmap --from-file=nutcracker.yaml twem-config`.

Finally, all of the preparations are done, and we can deploy our ambassador example. We define a pod that looks like this:

```
apiVersion: v1
kind: Pod
metadata:
  name: sharded-memcache-ambassador
spec:
  containers:
    # This is where the application container would go, for example
    # - name: nginx
    #   image: nginx
    # This is the ambassador container
    - name: twemproxy
      image: ganomede/twemproxy
      command:
      - nutcracker
      - -c
      - /etc/config/nutcracker.yaml
      - -v
      - 7
      - -s
      - 6222
      volumeMounts:
      - name: config-volume
        mountPath: /etc/config
  volumes:
    - name: config-volume
      configMap:
        name: twem-config
```

You can save this to a file named *memcached-ambassador-pod.yaml*, and then deploy it with:

```
kubectl create -f memcached-ambassador-pod.yaml
```

Of course, we don't have to use the ambassador pattern if we don't want to. An alternative is to deploy a replicated *shard router* service. There are trade-offs between using an ambassador versus using a shard routing service. The value of the service is a reduction of complexity. You don't have to deploy the ambassador with every pod that wants to access the sharded memcache service, it can be accessed via a named and load-balanced service. The downside of a shared service is twofold. First, because it is a shared service, you will have to scale it larger as demand load increases. Second, using the shared service introduces an extra network hop that will add some latency to requests and contribute network bandwith to the overall distributed system.

To deploy a shared routing service, you need to change the twemproxy configuration slightly so that it listens on all interfaces, not just localhost:

```
memcache:
  listen: 0.0.0.0:11211
  hash: fnv1a_64
  distribution: ketama
  auto_eject_hosts: true
  timeout: 400
  server_retry_timeout: 2000
  server_failure_limit: 1
  servers:
   - memcache-0.memcache:11211:1
   - memcache-1.memcache:11211:1
   - memcache-2.memcache:11211:1
```

You can save this to a file named *shared-nutcracker.yaml*, and then create a corresponding `ConfigMap` using `kubectl`:

```
kubectl create configmap --from-file=shared-nutcracker.yaml shared-twem-config
```

Then you can turn up the replicated shard routing service as a `Deployment`:

```
apiVersion: extensions/v1beta1
kind: Deployment
metadata:
  name: shared-twemproxy
spec:
  replicas: 3
  template:
    metadata:
      labels:
        app: shared-twemproxy
    spec:
      containers:
      - name: twemproxy
        image: ganomede/twemproxy
```

```
      command:
      - nutcracker
      - -c
      - /etc/config/shared-nutcracker.yaml
      - -v
      - 7
      - -s
      - 6222
      volumeMounts:
      - name: config-volume
        mountPath: /etc/config
    volumes:
    - name: config-volume
      configMap:
        name: shared-twem-config
```

If you save this to *shared-twemproxy-deploy.yaml*, you can create the replicated shard router using kubectl:

```
kubectl create -f shared-twemproxy-deploy.yaml
```

To complete the shard router, we have to declare a load balancer to process requests:

```
kind: Service
apiVersion: v1
metadata:
  name: shard-router-service
spec:
  selector:
    app: shared-twemproxy
  ports:
    - protocol: TCP
      port: 11211
      targetPort: 11211
```

This load balancer can be created using kubectl create -f shard-router-service.yaml.

An Examination of Sharding Functions

So far we've discussed the design and deployment of both simple sharded and replicated sharded caches, but we haven't spent very much time considering how traffic is routed to different shards. Consider a sharded service where you have 10 independent shards. Given some specific user request *Req*, how do you determine which shard *S* in the range from zero to nine should be used for the request? This mapping is the responsibility of the *sharding function*. A sharding function is very similar to a hashing function, which you may have encountered when learning about hashtable data structures. Indeed, a bucket-based hashtable could be considered an example of a sharded service. Given both *Req* and *Shard*, then the role of the sharding function is to relate them together, specifically:

$Shard = ShardingFunction(Req)$

Commonly, the sharding function is defined using a *hashing function* and the modulo (%) operator. Hashing functions are functions that transform an arbitrary object into an integer *hash*. The hash function has two important characteristics for our sharding:

Determinism
> The output should always be the same for a unique input.

Uniformity
> The distribution of outputs across the output space should be equal.

For our sharded service, determinism and uniformity are the most important characteristics. Determinism is important because it ensures that a particular request *R* always goes to the same shard in the service. Uniformity is important because it ensures that load is evenly spread between the different shards.

Fortunately for us, modern programming languages include a wide variety of high-quality hash functions. However, the outputs of these hash functions are often significantly larger than the number of shards in a sharded service. Consequently, we use the modulo operator (%) to reduce a hash function to the appropriate range. Returning to our sharded service with 10 shards, we can see that we can define our sharding function as:

$Shard = hash(Req) \% 10$

If the output of the hash function has the appropriate properties in terms of determinism and uniformity, those properties will be preserved by the modulo operator.

Selecting a Key

Given this sharding function, it might be tempting to simply use the hashing function that is built into the programming language, hash the entire object, and call it a day. The result of this, however, will not be a very good sharding function.

To understand this, consider a simple HTTP request that contains three things:

- The time of the request
- The source IP address from the client
- The HTTP request path (e.g., */some/page.html*)

If we use a simple object-based hashing function, `shard(request)`, then it is clear that `{12:00, 1.2.3.4, /some/file.html}` has a different shard value than `{12:01,`

`5.6.7.8, /some/file.html`}. The output of the sharding function is different because the client's IP address and the time of the request are different between the two requests. But of course, in most cases, the IP address of the client and the time of the request don't impact the response to the HTTP request. Consequently, instead of hashing the entire request object, a much better sharding function would be `shard(request.path)`. When we use `request.path` as the shard key, then we map both requests to the same shard, and thus the response to one request can be served out of the cache to service the other.

Of course, sometimes client IP *is* important to the response that is returned from the frontend. For example, client IP may be used to look up the geographic region that the user is located in, and different content (e.g., different languages) may be returned to different IP addresses. In such cases, the previous sharding function `shard(request.path)` will actually result in errors, since a cache request from a French IP address may be served a result page from the cache in English. In such cases, the cache function is too *general*, as it groups together requests that do not have identical responses.

Given this problem, it would be tempting then to define our sharding function as `shard(request.ip, request.path)`, but this sharding function has problems as well. It will cause two different French IP addresses to map to different shards, thus resulting in inefficient sharding. This shard function is too *specific*, as it fails to group together requests that are identical. A better sharding function for this situation would be:

```
shard(country(request.ip), request.path)
```

This first determines the country from the IP address, and then uses that country as part of the key for the sharding function. Thus multiple requests from France will be routed to one shard, while requests from the United States will be routed to a different shard.

Determining the appropriate key for your sharding function is vital to designing your sharded system well. Determining the correct shard key requires an understanding of the requests that you expect to see.

Consistent Hashing Functions

Setting up the initial shards for a new service is relatively straightforward: you set up the appropriate shards and the roots to perform the sharding, and you are off to the races. However, what happens when you need to change the number of shards in your sharded service? Such "re-sharding" is often a complicated process.

To understand why this is true, consider the sharded cache previously examined. Certainly, scaling the cache from 10 to 11 replicas is straightforward to do with a container orchestrator, but consider the effect of changing the scaling function from *hash(Req) % 10* to *hash(Req) % 11*. When you deploy this new scaling function, a large number of requests are going to be mapped to a different shard than the one they were previously mapped to. In a sharded cache, this is going to dramatically increase your *miss rate* until the cache is repopulated with responses for the new requests that have been mapped to that cache shard by the new sharding function. In the worst case, rolling out a new sharding function for your sharded cache will be equivalent to a complete cache failure.

To resolve these kinds of problems, many sharding functions use *consistent hashing functions*. Consistent hashing functions are special hash functions that are guaranteed to only remap *# keys / # shards*, when being resized to *# shards*. For example, if we use a consistent hashing function for our sharded cache, moving from 10 to 11 shards will only result in remapping < 10% (*K / 11*) keys. This is dramatically better than losing the entire sharded service.

Hands On: Building a Consistent HTTP Sharding Proxy

To shard HTTP requests, the first question to answer is what to use as the key for the sharding function. Though there are several options, a good general-purpose key is the request path as well as the fragment and query parameters (i.e., everything that makes the request unique). Note that this does *not* include cookies from the user or the language/location (e.g., EN_US). If your service provides extensive customization to users or their location, you will need to include them in the hash key as well.

We can use the versatile nginx HTTP server for our sharding proxy.

```
worker_processes  5;
error_log  error.log;
pid        nginx.pid;
worker_rlimit_nofile 8192;

events {
  worker_connections  1024;
}

http {
    # define a named 'backend' that we can use in the proxy directive
    # below.
    upstream backend {
        # Has the full URI of the request and use a consistent hash
        hash $request_uri consistent
        server web-shard-1.web;
        server web-shard-2.web;
        server web-shard-3.web;
    }

    server {
```

```
        listen localhost:80;
        location / {
            proxy_pass http://backend;
        }
    }
}
```

Note that we chose to use the full request URI as the key for the hash and use the key word `consistent` to indicate that we want to use a consistent hashing function.

Sharded, Replicated Serving

Most of the examples in this chapter so far have described sharding in terms of cache serving. But, of course, caches are not the only kinds of services that can benefit from sharding. Sharding is useful when considering any sort of service where there is more data than can fit on a single machine. In contrast to previous examples, the key and sharding function are not a part of the HTTP request, but rather some context for the user.

For example, consider implementing a large-scale multi-player game. Such a game world is likely to be far too large to fit on a single machine. However, players who are distant from each other in this virtual world are unlikely to interact. Consequently, the world of the game can be *sharded* across many different machines. The sharding function is keyed off of the player's location so that all players in a particular location land on the same set of servers.

Hot Sharding Systems

Ideally the load on a sharded cache will be perfectly even, but in many cases this isn't true and "hot shards" appear because organic load patterns drive more traffic to one particular shard.

As an example of this, consider a sharded cache for a user's photos; when a particular photo goes viral and suddenly receives a disproportionate amount of traffic, the cache shard containing that photo will become "hot." When this happens, with a replicated, sharded cache, you can scale the cache shard to respond to the increased load. Indeed, if you set up autoscaling for each cache shard, you can dynamically grow and shrink each replicated shard as the organic traffic to your service shifts around. An illustration of this process is shown in Figure 6-3. Initially the sharded service receives equal traffic to all three shards. Then the traffic shifts so that Shard A is receiving four times as much traffic as Shard B and Shard C. The hot sharding system moves Shard B to the same machine as Shard C, and replicates Shard A to a second machine. Traffic is now, once again, equally shared between replicas.

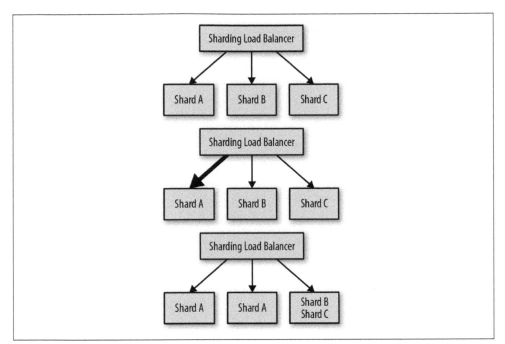

Figure 6-3. An example of a hot sharded system: initially the shards are evenly distributed, but when extra traffic comes to shard A, it is replicated to two machines, and shards B and C are combined on a single machine

## CHAPTER 7

Scatter/Gather

So far we've examined systems that replicate for scalability in terms of the number of requests processed per second (the stateless replicated pattern), as well as scalability for the size of the data (the sharded data pattern). In this chapter we introduce the *scatter/gather* pattern, which uses replication for scalability in terms of time. Specifically, the scatter/gather pattern allows you to achieve parallelism in servicing requests, enabling you to service them significantly faster than you could if you had to service them sequentially.

Like replicated and sharded systems, the scatter/gather pattern is a tree pattern with a root that distributes requests and leaves that process those requests. However, in contrast to replicated and sharded systems, with scatter/gather requests are simultaneously farmed out to all of the replicas in the system. Each replica does a small amount of processing and then returns a fraction of the result to the root. The root server then combines the various partial results together to form a single complete response to the request and then sends this request back out to the client. The scatter/gather pattern is illustrated in Figure 7-1.

Scatter/gather is quite useful when you have a large amount of mostly independent processing that is needed to handle a particular request. Scatter/gather can be seen as sharding the computation necessary to service the request, rather than sharding the data (although data sharding may be part of it as well).

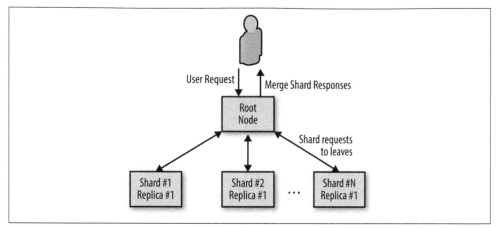

Figure 7-1. A scatter/gather pattern

Scatter/Gather with Root Distribution

The simplest form of scatter/gather is one in which each leaf is entirely homogenous but the work is distributed to a number of different leaves in order to improve the performance of the request. This pattern is equivalent to solving an "embarassingly parallel" problem. The problem can be broken up into many different pieces and each piece can be put back together with all of the other pieces to form a complete answer.

To understand this in more concrete terms, imagine that you need to service a user request R and it takes one minute for a single core to produce the answer A to this request. If we program a multi-threaded application, we can parallelize this request on a single machine by using multiple cores. Given this approach and a 30 core processor (yes, typically it would be a 32 core processor, but 30 makes the math cleaner), we can reduce the time that it takes to process a single request down to 2 seconds (60 seconds of computation split across 30 threads for computation is equal to 2 seconds). But even two seconds is pretty slow to service a user's web request. Additionally, truly achieving a completely parallel speed up on a single process is going to be tricky as things like memory, network, or disk bandwidth start to become the bottleneck. Instead of parallelizing an application across cores on a single machine, we can use the scatter/gather pattern to parallelize requests across multiple processes on many different machines. In this way, we can improve our overall latency requests, since we are no longer bound by the number of cores we can get on a single machine, as well as ensure that the bottleneck in our process continues to be CPU, since the memory, network, and disk bandwidth are all spread across a number of different machines. Additionally, because every machine in the scatter/gather tree is capable of handling every request, the root of the tree can dynamically dispatch load to different nodes at different times depending on their responsiveness. If, for some reason, a particular leaf node is responding more slowly than other machines (e.g., it has a noisy neighbor process that is interfering with resources), then the root can dynamically redistribute load to assure a fast response.

Hands On: Distributed Document Search

To see an example of scatter/gather in action, consider the task of searching across a large database of documents for all documents that contain the words "cat" and "dog." One way to perform this search would be to open up all of the documents, read through the entire set, searching for the words in each document, and then return to the user the set of documents that contain both words.

As you might imagine, this is quite a slow process because it requires opening and reading through a large number of files for each request. To make request processing faster, you can build an *index*. The index is effectively a hashtable, where the keys are individual words (e.g., "cat") and the values are a list of documents containing that word.

Now, instead of searching through every document, finding the documents that match any one word is as easy as doing a lookup in this hashtable. However, we have lost one important ability. Remember that we were looking for all documents that contained "cat" *and* "dog." Since the index only has single words, not conjunctions of words, we still need to find the documents that contain both words. Luckily, this is just an intersection of the sets of documents returned for each word.

Given this approach, we can implement this document search as an example of the scatter/gather pattern. When a request comes in to the document search root, it parses the request and farms out two leaf machines (one for the word "cat" and one for the word "dog"). Each of these machines returns a list of documents that match one of the words, and the root node returns the list of documents containing both "cat" and "dog."

A diagram of this process is shown in Figure 7-2: the leaf returns {doc1, doc2, doc4} for "cat" and {doc1, doc3, doc4} for "dog," so the root finds the intersection and returns {doc1, doc4}.

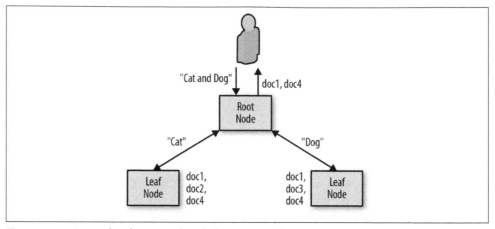

Figure 7-2. Example of a term-sharded scatter/gather system

Scatter/Gather with Leaf Sharding

While applying the replicated data scatter/gather pattern allows you to reduce the processing time required for handling user requests, it doesn't allow you to scale beyond an amount of data that can be held in the memory or disk of a single machine. Much like the replicated serving pattern that was previously described, it is simple to build a replicated scatter/gather system. But at a certain data size, it is necessary to introduce sharding in order to build a system that can hold more data than can be stored on a single machine.

Previously, when sharding was introduced to scale replicated systems, the sharding was done at a per-request level. Some part of the request was used to determine where the request was sent. That replica then handled all of the processing for the request and the response was handed back to the user. Instead, with scatter/gather sharding, the request is sent to all of the leaf nodes (or shards) in the system. Each leaf node processes the request using the data that it has loaded in its shard. This partial response is then returned to the root node that requested data, and that root node merges all of the responses together to form a comprehensive response for the user.

As a concrete example of this sort of architecture, consider implementing search across a very large document set (all patents in the world, for example); in such a case, the data is too large to fit in the memory of a single machine, so instead the data is sharded across multiple replicas. For example, patents 0-100,000 might be on the first machine, 100,001-200,000 on the next machine, and so forth. (Note that this is not actually a good sharding scheme since it will continually force us to add new shards as new patents are registered. In practice, we'd likely use the patent number modulo the total number of shards.) When a user submits a request to find a particular word (e.g., "rockets") in all of the patents in the index, that request is sent to each shard, which searches through it's patent shard for patents which match the word in the query. Any matches that are found are returned to the root node in response to the shard request. The root node then collates all of these responses together into a single response that contains all the patents that match the particular word. The operation of this search index is illustrated in Figure 7-3.

Hands On: Sharded Document Search

The previous example scattered the different term requests across the cluster, but this only works if all of the documents are present on all of the machines in the scatter/ gather tree. If there is not enough room for all of the documents in all of the leaves in the tree, then sharding must be used to put different sets of documents onto different leaves.

This means that when a user makes a request for all documents that match the words "cat" and "dog," the request is actually sent out to every leaf in the scatter/gather system. Each leaf node returns the set of documents that it knows about that matches "cat" and "dog." Previously, the root node was responsible for performing the intersection of the two sets of documents returned for two different words. In the sharded case, the root node is responsible for generating the union of all of the documents returned by all of the different shards and returning this complete set of documents back up to the user.

In Figure 7-3, the first leaf serves documents 1 through 10 and returns {doc1, doc5}. The second leaf serves documents 11 through 20 and returns {doc15}. The third leaf serves documents 21 through 30 and returns {doc22, doc28}. The root combines all of these responses together into a single response and returns {doc1, doc5, doc15, doc22, doc28}.

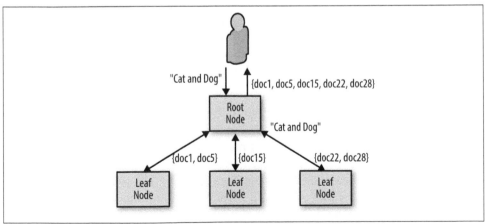

Figure 7-3. Conjunctive query executing in a scatter/gather search system

Choosing the Right Number of Leaves

It might seem that in the scatter/gather pattern, replicating out to a very large number of leaves would always be a good idea. You parallelize your computation and consequently reduce the clock time required to process any particular request. However, increased parallelization comes at a cost, and thus choosing the right number of leaf nodes in the scatter/gather pattern is critical to designing a performant distributed system.

To understand how this can happen, it's worth considering two things. The first is that processing any particular request has a certain amount of overhead. This is the time spent parsing a request, sending HTTP across the wire, and so forth. In general, the overhead due to system request handling is constant and significantly less than the time spent in user code processing the request. Consequently, this overhead can generally be ignored when assessing the performance of the scatter/gather pattern. However, it is important to understand that the cost of this overhead scales with the number of leaf nodes in the scatter/gather pattern. Thus, even though it is low cost, as parallelization continues, this overhead eventually dominates the compute cost of your business logic. This means that the gains of parallelization are asymptotic.

In addition to the fact that adding more leaf nodes may not actually speed up processing, scatter/gather systems also suffer from the "straggler" problem. To understand how this works, it is important to remember that in a scatter/gather system, the root node waits for requests from *all* of the leaf nodes to return before sending a response back to the end user. Since data from every leaf node is required, the overall time it takes to process a user request is defined by the slowest leaf node that sends a response. To understand the impact of this, imagine that we have a service that has a 99th percentile latency of 2 seconds. This means that on average one request out of every 100 has a latency of 2 seconds, or put another way, there is a 1% chance that a request will take 2 seconds. This may be totally acceptable at first glance: a single user out of 100 has a slow request. However, consider how this actually works in a scatter/gather system. Since the time of the user request is defined by the slowest response, we need to consider not a single request but all requests scattered out to the various leaf nodes.

Let's see what happens when we scatter out to five leaf nodes. In this situation, there is a 5% chance that one of these five scatter requests has a latency of 2 seconds (0.99 × 0.99 × 0.99 × 0.99 × 0.99 == 0.95). This means that our 99th percentile latency for individual requests becomes a 95th percentile latency for our complete scatter/gather system. And it only gets worse from there: if we scatter out to 100 leaves, then we are more or less guaranteeing that our overall latency for *all* requests will be 2 seconds.

Together, these complications of scatter/gather systems lead us to some conclusions:

- Increased parallelism doesn't always speed things up because of overhead on each node.
- Increased parallelism doesn't always speed things up because of the straggler problem.
- The performance of the 99th percentile is more important than in other systems because each user request actually becomes numerous requests to the service.

The same straggler problem applies to availability. If you issue a request to 100 leaf nodes, and the probability that any leaf node failing is 1 in 100, you are again practically guaranteed to fail every single user request.

Scaling Scatter/Gather for Reliability and Scale

Of course, just as with a sharded system, having a single replica of a sharded scatter/gather system is likely not the desirable design choice. A single replica means that if it fails, all scatter/gather requests will fail for the duration that the shard is unavailable because all requests are required to be processed by all leaf nodes in the scatter/gather pattern. Likewise, upgrades will take out a percentage of your shards, so an upgrade while under user-facing load is no longer possible. Finally, the computational scale of your system will be limited by the load that any single node is capable of achieving. Ultimately, this limits your scale, and as we have seen in previous sections, you cannot simply increase the number of shards in order to improve the computational power of a scatter/gather pattern.

Given these challenges of reliability and scale, the correct approach is to replicate each of the individual shards so that instead of a single instance at each leaf node, there is a replicated service that implements each leaf shard. This replicated, sharded scatter/gather pattern is shown in Figure 7-4.

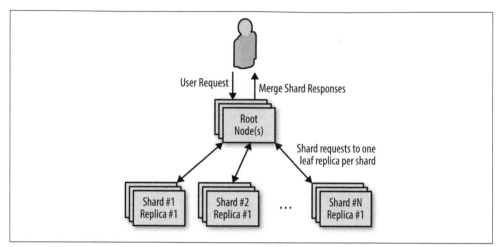

Figure 7-4. A sharded, replicated scatter/gatther system

Built this way, each leaf request from the root is actually load balanced across all healthy replicas of the shard. This means that if there are any failures, they won't result in a user-visible outage for your system. Likewise, you can safely perform an upgrade under load, since each replicated shard can be upgraded one replica at a time. Indeed, you can perform the upgrade across multiple shards simultaneously, depending on how quickly you want to perform the upgrade.

## CHAPTER 8

Functions and Event-Driven Processing

So far, we have examined design for systems with long-running computation. The servers that handle user requests are always up and running. This pattern is the right one for many applications that are under heavy load, keep a large amount of data in memory, or require some sort of background processing. However, there is a class of applications that might only need to temporarily come into existence to handle a single request, or simply need to respond to a specific event. This style of request or event-driven application design has flourished recently as large-scale public cloud providers have developed *function-as-a-service* (FaaS) products. More recently, FaaS implementations have also emerged running on top of cluster orchestrators in private cloud or physical environments. This chapter describes emerging architectures for this new style of computing. In many cases, FaaS is a component in a broader architecture rather than a complete solution.

 Oftentimes, FaaS is referred to as *serverless* computing. And while this is true (you don't see the servers in FaaS) it's worth differentiating between event-driven FaaS and the broader notion of serverless computing. Indeed, serverless computing can apply to a wide variety of computing services; for example, a multi-tenant container orchestrator (container-as-a-service) is serverless but not event-driven. Conversely, an open source FaaS running on a cluster of physical machines that you own and administer is event-driven but not serverless. Understanding this distinction enables you to determine when event-driven, serverless, or both is the right choice for your application.

Determining When FaaS Makes Sense

As with many tools for developing a distributed system, it can be tempting to see a particular solution like event-driven processing as a universal hammer. However, the truth is that it is best suited to a particular set of problems. Within a particular context it is a powerful tool, but stretching it to fit all applications or systems will lead to overly complicated, brittle designs. Especially since FaaS is such a new computing tool, before discussing specific design patterns, it is worth discussing the benefits, limitations, and optimal situations for employing event-driven computing.

The Benefits of FaaS

The benefits of FaaS are primarily for the developer. It dramatically simplifies the distance from code to running service. Because there is no artifact to create or push beyond the source code itself, FaaS makes it simple to go from code on a laptop or web browser to running code in the cloud.

Likewise, the code that is deployed is managed and scaled automatically. As more traffic is loaded onto the service, more instances of the function are created to handle that increase in traffic. If a function fails due to application or machine failures, it is automatically restarted on some other machine.

Finally, much like containers, functions are an even more granular building block for designing distributed systems. Functions are stateless and thus any system you build on top of functions is inherently more modular and decoupled than a similar system built into a single binary. But, of course, this is also the challenge of developing systems in FaaS. The decoupling is both a strength and a weakness. The following section describes some of the challenges that come from developing systems using FaaS.

The Challenges of FaaS

As described in the previous section, developing systems using FaaS forces you to strongly decouple each piece of your service. Each function is entirely independent. The only communication is across the network, and each function instance cannot have local memory, requiring all states to be stored in a storage service. This forced decoupling can improve the agility and speed with which you can develop services, but it can also significantly complicate the operations of the same service.

In particular, it is often quite difficult to obtain a comprehensive view of your service, determine how the various functions integrate with one another, and understand when things go wrong, and why they go wrong. Additionally, the request-based and serverless nature of functions means that certain problems are quite difficult to detect. As an example, consider the following functions:

- *functionA()* which calls *functionB()*
- *functionB()* which calls *functionC()*
- *functionC()* which calls back to *functionA()*

Now consider what happens when a request comes into any of these functions: it kicks off an infinite loop that only terminates when the original request times out (and possibly not even then) or when you run out of money to pay for requests in the system. Obviously, the above example is quite contrived, but it is actually quite difficult to detect in your code. Since each function is radically decoupled from the other functions, there is no real representation of the dependencies or interactions between different functions. These problems are not unsolvable, and I expect that as FaaSs mature, more analysis and debugging tools will provide a richer experience to understand how and why an application comprised of FaaS is performing the way that it does.

For now, when adopting FaaS, you must be vigilant to adopt rigorous monitoring and alerting for how your system is behaving so that you can detect situations and correct them before they become significant problems. Of course, the complexity introduced by monitoring flies somewhat in the face of the simplicity of deploying to FaaS, which is friction that your developers must overcome.

The Need for Background Processing

FaaS is inherently an event-based application model. Functions are executed in response to discrete events that occur and trigger the execution of the functions. Additionally, because of the serverless nature of the implementation of theses services, the runtime of any particular function instance is generally time bounded. This means that FaaS is usually a poor fit for situations that require processing. Examples of such background processing might be transcoding a video, compressing log files, or other sorts of low-priority, long-running computations. In many cases, it is possible to set up a scheduled trigger that synthetically generates events in your functions on a particular schedule. Though this is a good fit for responding to temporal events (e.g., firing a text-message alarm to wake someone up), it is still not sufficient infrastructure for generic background processing. To achieve that, you need to launch your code in an environment that supports long-running processes. And this generally means switching to a pay-per-consumption rather than pay-per-request model for the parts of your application that do background processing.

The Need to Hold Data in Memory

In addition to the operational challenges, there are some architectural limitations that make FaaS ill-suited for some types of applications. The first of these limitations is the need to have a significant amount of data loaded into memory in order to process user requests. There are a variety of services (e.g., serving a search index of documents) that require a great deal of data to be loaded in memory in order to service user requests. Even with a relatively fast storage layer, loading such data can take significantly longer than the desired time to service a user request. Because with FaaS, the function itself may be dynamically spun up in response to a user request *while the user is waiting*, the need to load a lot of detail may significantly impact the latency that the user perceives while interacting with your service. Of course, once your FaaS has been created, it may handle a large number of requests, so this loading cost can be amortized across a large number of requests. But if you have a sufficient number of requests to keep a function active, then it's likely you are overpaying for the requests you are processing.

The Costs of Sustained Request-Based Processing

The cost model of public cloud FaaS is based on per-request pricing. This approach is great if you only have a few requests per minute or hour. In such a situation, you are idle most of the time, and given a pay-per-request model, you are only paying for the time when your service is actively serving requests. In contrast, if you service requests via a long-running service either in a container or a virtual machine, then you are always paying for processor cycles that is largely sitting around waiting for a user request.

However, as a service grows, the number of requests that you are servicing grows to the point where you can keep a processor continuously active servicing user requests. At this point, the economics of a pay-per-request model start to become bad, and only get worse because the cost of cloud virtual machines generally decreases as you add more cores (and also via committed resources like reservations or sustained use discounts), whereas the cost per-request largely grows linearly with the number of requests.

Consequently, as your service grows and evolves, it's highly likely that your use of FaaS will evolve as well. One ideal way to scale FaaS is to run an open source FaaS that runs on a container orchestrator like Kubernetes. That way, you can still take advantage of the developer benefits of FaaS, while taking advantage of the pricing models of virtual machines.

Patterns for FaaS

In addition to understanding the trade-offs in deploying event-driven or FaaS architectures as part of your distributed system, understanding the best ways to deploy FaaS is critical to the design of a successful system. This section describes some canonical patterns for incorporating FaaS.

The Decorator Pattern: Request or Response Transformation

FaaS is ideal for deploying simple functions that can take an input, transform it into an output, and then pass it on to a different service. This general pattern can be used to augment or decorate HTTP requests to or from a different service. A basic illustration of this pattern is shown in Figure 8-1.

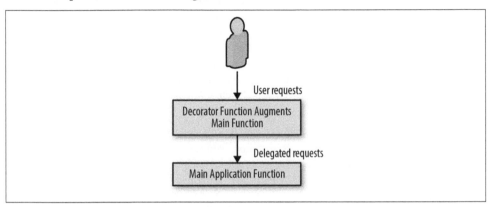

Figure 8-1. The decorator pattern applied to HTTP APIs

Interestingly, there are several analogies to this pattern in programming languages. In particular, the *decorator* pattern from Python is a close analogue for the services that a request or response decorator can perform. Because decoration transformations are generally stateless, and also because they are often added after the fact to existing code as the service evolves, they are ideal services to implement via FaaS. Additionally, the lightness of FaaS means that you can experiment with a variety of different decorators before finally adopting one and pulling it more completely into the implementation of the service.

A great example of the value of the decorator pattern is adding defaults to the input to an HTTP RESTFul API. In many cases in the API, there are fields whose values should have sane defaults if they are left empty. For example, you may want a field to default to true, but it's difficult to accomplish this in classical JSON, because the default value for a field is null, which is generally understood to be false. To resolve this, we can add defaulting logic either in the front of the API server or within the application code itself (e.g., if (field == null) field = true). However, both of these solutions are somewhat unappealing since the defaulting mechanism is fairly conceptually independent from the handling of the request. Instead, we can use the FaaS decorator pattern to transform the request in between the user and the service implementation.

Given the previous discussion of the adapter pattern in the single-node section, you may be wondering why we don't simply package this defaulting as an adapter container. And this is a totally reasonable approach, but it does mean that we are going to couple the scale of the defaulting service with the API service itself. The defaulting is actually a lightweight operation, and we are likely to need far fewer instances of it than the service itself to handle the load.

 For the examples in this chapter, we are going to use the kubeless (*https://github.com/kubeless/kubeless*) FaaS framework. Kubeless is deployed on top of the Kubernetes container orchestration service. Assuming that you have provisioned a Kubernetes cluster, you can install Kubeless from its releases page (*https://github.com/kubeless/ kubeless/releases*). Once you have the kubeless binary installed, you can install it into your cluster with the following commands: kubeless install.

Kubeless installs itself as a native Kubernetes third-party API. This means that once it is installed, you can use the native kubectl command-line tool. For example, you can see deployed functions using kubectl get functions. Currently, you should have no functions deployed.

Hands On: Adding Request Defaulting Prior to Request Processing

To demonstrate the utility of the decorator pattern for FaaS, consider the task of adding default values to a RESTful function call if the values are missing. This is quite straightforward to do using FaaS. We'll write the defaulting function using the Python programming language:

```
# Simple handler function for adding default values
def handler(context):
  # Get the input value
  obj = context.json
  # If the 'name' field is not present, set it randomly
  if obj.get("name", None) is None:
    obj["name"] = random_name()
  # If the 'color' field is not present, set it to 'blue'
  if obj.get("color", None) is None:
    obj["color"] = "blue"
  # Call the actual API, potentially with the new default
  # values, and return the result
  return call_my_api(obj)
```

Save this function in a file named *defaults.py*. You obviously will want to update the call_my_api code so that it points to the actual API you want to call. Once you have finished writing the code, this defaulting function can be installed as a kubeless function using:

```
kubeless function deploy add-defaults \
    --runtime python27 \
```

```
--handler defaults.handler \
--from-file defaults.py \
--trigger-http
```

If you want to test the handling of this function, you can also use the `kubeless` tool:

```
kubeless function call add-defaults --data '{"name": "foo"}'
```

The decorator pattern shows just how easy it is to adapt and extend existing APIs with additional features like validation or defaulting.

Handling Events

While most systems are request driven, handling a steady stream of user and API requests, many other systems are more event-driven in nature. The differentiation, in my mind at least, between a request and an event have to do with the notion of *session*. Requests are part of a larger series of interactions or sessions; generally each user request is part of a larger interaction with a complete web application or API. *Events*, as I see them, instead tend to be single-instance and asynchronous in nature. Events are important and need to be properly handled, but they are fired off from a main interaction and responded to some time later. Examples of events include a user signing up for a new service (which might trigger a welcome email, someone uploading a file to a shared folder (which might send notifications to everyone who has access to the folder), or even a machine being about to reboot (which might notify an operator or automated system to take appropriate action).

Because these events tend to be largely independent and stateless in nature, and because the rate of events can be highly variable, they are ideal candidates for event-driven and FaaS architectures. In this role, they are often deployed alongside a production application server as augmentation to the main user experience, or to handle some sort of reactive, background processing. Additionally, because new events are often dynamically added to the service, the lightweight nature of deploying functions is a good match for defining new event handlers. Likewise, because each event is conceptually independent, the forced decoupling of a functions-based system actually helps *reduce* the conceptual complexity by enabling a developer to focus on the steps required to handle just a single type of event.

A concrete example of integrating an event-based component to an existing service is implementing two-factor authentication. In this case, the event is the user logging into a service. The service can generate an event for this action, fire it into a function-based handler that takes the code and the user's contact information, and sends the two-factor code via text message.

Hands On: Implementing Two-Factor Authentication

Two-factor authentication requires that the user both have something that they know (e.g., a password) as well as something that they possess (e.g., a phone) to be able to log in to the system. Two-factor authentication is significantly more secure than passwords alone since it requires two different security compromises (a thief learning your password *and* a thief stealing your phone) to enable a true security problem.

When considering how to implement two-factor authentication, one of the challenges is how to handle the request to generate a random code and register it with the login service as well as send the text message. It is possible to add this code to the main login web server. But it is complicated and monolithic, and forces the act of sending a text message, which can have some latency, to be inline with the code that renders the login web page. This latency produces a substandard user experience.

A better option is to register a FaaS to asynchronously generate the random number, register it with the login service, and send the number to the user's phone. In this way, the login server can simply fire an asynchronous web-hook request to a FaaS, and that FaaS can handle the somewhat slow and asynchronous task of registering the two-factor code and sending the text message.

To see how this works in practice, consider the following code:

```
def two_factor(context):
    # Generate a random six digit code
    code = random.randint(100000, 999999)

    # Register the code with the login service
    user = context.json["user"]
    register_code_with_login_service(user, code)

    # Use the twillio library to send texts
    account = "my-account-sid"
    token = "my-token"
    client = twilio.rest.Client(account, token)

    user_number = context.json["phoneNumber"]
    msg = "Hello {} your authentication code is: {}.".format(user, code)
    message = client.api.account.messages.create(to=user_number,
                                                 from_="+12065251212",
                                                 body=msg)
    return {"status": "ok"}
```

We can then register this FaaS with kubeless:

```
kubeless function deploy add-two-factor \
    --runtime python27 \
    --handler two_factor.two_factor \
    --from-file two_factor.py \
    --trigger-http
```

This function can then be made asynchronously from client-side JavaScript whenever the user successfully provides their password. The web UX can then immediately display a page to enter the code, and the user (once they receive the code as a text message) can supply it to the service, where the code has already been registered via our FaaS.

Again, developing a simple, asynchronous, event-based service that is triggered whenever a user logs in is made dramatically simpler using FaaS.

Event-Based Pipelines

There are some applications that are inherently easier to think about in terms of a pipeline of decoupled events. These event pipelines often resemble the flowcharts of old. They can be represented as a directed graph of connected event syncs. In the event pipeline pattern, each node is a different function or webhook, and the edges linking the graph together are HTTP or other network calls to the function/webhook. In general, there is no shared state between the different pieces of the pipeline, but there may be a context or other reference point that can be used to look up information in shared storage.

So what is the difference between this type of pipeline and a "microservices" architecture? There are two central differences. The first is the main difference between functions in general and long-running services, which is that an event-based pipeline is by its very nature event-driven. Conversely, a microservices architecture features a collection of long-running services. Additionally, event-driven pipelines may be highly asynchronous and diverse in the things that they connect together. For example, while it is difficult to see how a human approving a ticket in a ticketing system like Jira could be integrated into a microservices application, it's quite easy to see how that event could be incorporated into a event-driven pipeline.

As an example of this, imagine a pipeline in which the original event is code being submitted into a source control system. This event then triggers a build. The build may take multiple minutes to complete, and when it does, it fires an event to a build analysis function. This function takes different actions if the build is successful or fails. If the build succeeded, a ticket is created for a human to approve it to be pushed to production. Once the ticket is closed, the act of closing is an event that triggers the actual push to production. If the build failed, a bug is filed on the failure, and the event pipeline terminates.

Hands On: Implementing a Pipeline for New-User Signup

Consider the task of implementing a new-user signup flow. When a new user account is created, there are certain things that are always done, such as sending a welcome email. And there are some things that are optionally done, such as registering a user to receive product updates (sometimes known as "spam") via their email.

One approach to implementing this logic would be to place everything into a single monolithic *user-creation* server. However, this factoring means that a single team owns the entirety of the user-creation service, and that the entire experience is deployed as a single service. Both of these mean that it is more difficult to perform experiments or make changes to the user experience.

Consider, instead, implementing the user login experience as an event pipeline with a series of FaaS. In this factoring, the user-creation function is actually unaware of the details of what happens on user login. Instead, the main user-creation service simply has two lists:

- A list of required actions (e.g., sending a welcome mail)
- A list of optional actions (e.g., subscribing the user to a mailing list)

Each of these actions is also implemented as a FaaS, and the list of actions is actually just a list of webhooks. Consequently, the main user creation function looks like this:

```
def create_user(context):
  # For required event handlers, call them universally
  for key, value in required.items():
    call_function(value.webhook, context.json)

  # For optional event handlers, check and call them
  # conditionally
  for key, value in optional.items():
    if context.json.get(key, None) is not None:
      call_function(value.webhook, context.json)
```

Now we can also use FaaS to implement each of these handlers:

```
def email_user(context):
  # Get the user name
  user = context.json['username']

  msg = 'Hello {} thanks for joining my awesome service!".format(user)

  send_email(msg, contex.json['email])


def subscribe_user(context):
  # Get the user name
  email = context.json['email']
  subscribe_user(email)
```

Factored in this way, each FaaS is simple, containing only a few lines of code and focused on implementing one specific piece of functionality. This microservices-based approach is simple to write but might lead to complexity if we actually had to deploy and manage three different microservices. This is where FaaS can shine, since it makes it trivially easy to host these small code snippets. Additionally, by visualizing our user-creation flow as an event-driven pipeline, it is also straightforward to have a high-level understanding of what exactly happens on user login, simply by following the flow of the context through the various functions in the pipeline.

## CHAPTER 9

Ownership Election

The previous patterns that we have seen have been about distributing requests in order to scale requests per second, the state being served, or the time to process a request. This final chapter on multi-node serving patterns is about how you scale assignment. In many different systems, there is a notion of *ownership* where a specific process owns a specific task. We have previously seen this in the context of sharded and hot-sharded systems where specific instances owned specific sections of the sharded key space.

In the context of a single server, ownership is generally straightforward to achieve because there is only a single application that is establishing ownership, and it can use well-established in-process locks to ensure that only a single actor owns a particular shard or context. However, restricting ownership to a single application limits scalability, since the task can't be replicated, and reliability, since if the task fails, it is unavailable for a period of time. Consequently, when ownership is required in your system, you need to develop a distributed system for establishing ownership.

A general diagram of distributed ownership is shown in Figure 9-1. In the diagram, there are three replicas that could be the owner or master. Initially, the first replica is the master. Then that replica fails, and replica number three then becomes the master. Finally, replica number one recovers and returns to the group, but replica three remains as the master/owner.

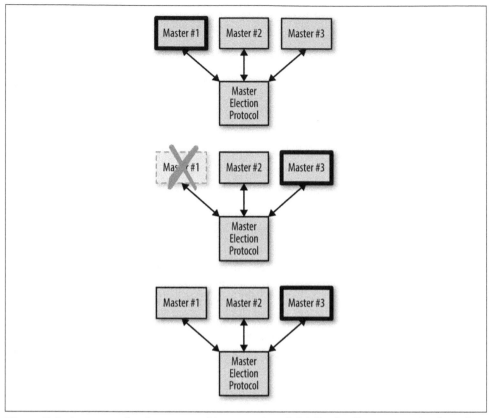

Figure 9-1. A master election protocol in operation: initially the first master is selected, but when it fails, the third master takes over

Often, establishing distributed ownership is both the most complicated and most important part of designing a reliable distributed system.

Determining If You Even Need Master Election

The simplest form of ownership is to just have a single replica of the service. Since there is only one instance running at a time, that instance implicitly owns everything without any need for election. This has advantages of simplifying your application and deployment, but it has disadvantages in terms of downtime and reliability. However, for many applications, the simplicity of this singleton pattern may be worth the reliability trade-off. Let's look at this further.

Assuming that you run your singleton in a container orchestration system like Kubernetes, you have the following guarantees:

- If the container crashes, it will automatically be restarted

- If the container hangs, and you implement a health check, it will automatically be restarted
- If the machine fails, the container will be moved to a different machine

Because of these guarantees, a singleton of a service running in a container orchestrator has pretty good uptime. To take the definition of "pretty good" a little further, let's examine what happens in each of these failure modes. If the container process fails or the container hangs, your application will be restarted in a few seconds. Assuming your container crashes once a day, this is roughly three to four nines of uptime (2 seconds of downtime / day ~= 99.99% uptime). If your container crashes less often, it's even better than that. If your machine fails, it takes a while for Kubernetes to decide that the machine has failed and move it over to a different machine; let's assume that takes around 5 minutes. Given that, if every machine in your cluster fails every day, then your service will have two nines of uptime. And honestly, if every machine in your cluster fails every day, then you have way worse problems than the uptime of your master-elected service.

It's worth considering, of course, that there are more reasons for downtime than just failures. When you are rolling out new software, it takes time to download and start the new version. With a singleton, you cannot have both old and new versions running at the same time, so you will need to take down the old version for the duration of the upgrade, which may be several minutes if your image is large. Consequently, if you deploy daily and it takes 2 minutes to upgrade your software, you will only be able to run a two nines service, and if you deploy hourly, it won't even be a single nine service. Of course, there are ways that you can speed up your deployment by pre-pulling the new image onto the machine before you run the update. This can reduce the time it takes to deploy a new version to a few seconds, but the trade-off is added complexity, which was what we were trying to avoid in the first place.

Regardless, there are many applications (e.g., background asynchronous processing) where such an SLA is an acceptable trade-off for application simplicity. One of the key components of designing a distributed system is deciding when the "distributed" part is actually unnecessarily complex. But there are certainly situations where high availability (four+ nines) is a critical component of the application, and in such systems you need to run multiple replicas of the service, where only one replica is the designated owner. The design of these types of systems is described in the sections that follow.

The Basics of Master Election

Imagine that there is a service *Foo* with three replicas: *Foo-1*, *Foo-2*, and *Foo-3*. There is also some object *Bar* that must only be "owned" by one of the replicas (e.g., *Foo-1*) at a time. Often this replica is called the *master*, hence the term *master election* used to describe the process of how this master is selected as well as how a new master is selected if that master fails.

There are two ways to implement this master election. This first is to implement a distributed consensus algorithm like Paxos or RAFT, but the complexity of these algorithms make them beyond the scope of this book and not worthwhile to implement. Implementing one of these algorithms is akin to implementing locks on top of assembly code compare-and-swap instructions. It's an interesting exercise for an undergraduate computer science course, but it is not something that is generally worth doing in practice.

Fortunately, there are a large number of distributed key-value stores that have implemented such consensus algorithms for you. At a general level, these systems provide a replicated, reliable data store and the primitives necessary to build more complicated locking and election abstractions on top. Examples of these distributed stores include etcd, ZooKeeper, and consul. The basic primitives that these systems provide is the ability to perform a compare-and-swap operation for a particular key. If you haven't seen compare-and-swap before, it is basically an atomic operation that looks like this:

```
var lock = sync.Mutex{}
var store = map[string]string{}

func compareAndSwap(key, nextValue, currentValue string) (bool, error) {
  lock.Lock()
  defer lock.Unlock()
  _, containsKey := store[key]
  if !containsKey {
    if len(currentValue) == 0 {
      store[key] = nextValue
      return true, nil
    }
    return false, fmt.Errorf("Expected value %s for key %s, but
    found empty", currentValue, key)
  }
  if store[key] == currentValue {
    store[key] = nextValue
    return true, nil
  }
  return false, nil
}
```

Compare-and-swap atomically writes a new value if the existing value matches the expected value. If the value doesn't match, it returns false. If the value doesn't exist and currentValue is not null, it returns an error.

In addition to compare-and-swap, the key-value stores allow you to set a time-to-live (TTL) for a key. Once the TTL expires, the key is set back to empty.

Put together, these functions are sufficient to implement a variety of distributed synchronization primitives.

Hands On: Deploying etcd

etcd (*https://coreos.com/etcd/docs/latest/*) is a distributed lock server developed by CoreOS. It is robust and proven in production at high scale, and is used by a variety of projects including Kubernetes.

Deploying etcd has fortunately become quite easy due to the development of two different open source projects:

- Helm (*https://helm.sh*): a Kubernetes package manager supported by Microsoft Azure
- The etcd operator (*https://coreos.com/blog/introducing-the-etcd-operator.html*) developed by CoreOS

 Operators are an interesting topic being explored by CoreOS. An operator is an online program that runs inside your container orchestrator with the express purpose of running one or more applications. The operator is responsible for creating, scaling, and maintaining the successful operation of the program. Users configure the application through a desired state API. For example, the etcd operator is in charge of monitoring etcd itself. Operators are still a new idea but represent an important new direction in building reliable distributed systems.

To deploy the etcd operator for CoreOS, we're going to use the helm package management tool. Helm is an open source package manager that is part of the Kubernetes project, and was developed by Deis. Deis was acquired by Microsoft Azure in 2017 and Microsoft continues to support the further open source development of Helm.

If this is your first time using helm, you need to install the helm tool, following the instructions here: *https://github.com/kubernetes/helm/releases*.

Once you have the helm tool installed in your environment, you can install the etcd operator using helm, as follows:

```
# Initialize helm
helm init

# Install the etcd operator
helm install stable/etcd-operator
```

Once the operator is installed, it creates a custom Kubernetes resource to represent the etcd cluster. The operator is running, but there are no etcd clusters yet. To create an etcd cluster, you need to create a declarative configuration:

```
apiVersion: "etcd.coreos.com/v1beta1"
kind: "Cluster"
metadata:
  # Whatever name you want here
  name: "my-etcd-cluster"
spec:
  # 1, 3, 5 are the options for size
  size: 3
  # The version of etcd to install
  version: "3.1.0"
```

Save this configuration to *etcd-cluster.yaml* and then create the cluster using `kubectl create -f etcd-cluster.yaml`.

Creating this cluster will cause the the operator to create pods for the replicas of the etcd cluster. You can see the running replicas using:

```
kubectl get pods
```

Once all three replicas are running, you can get their endpoints using:

```
export ETCD_ENDPOINTS=kubectl get endpoints example-etcd-cluster
"-o=jsonpath={.subsets[*].addresses[*].ip}:2379,"
```

You can then store something into etcd using:

```
kubectl exec my-etcd-cluster-0000 -- sh -c "ETCD_API=3 etcdctl
--endpoints=${ETCD_ENDPOINTS} set foo bar"
```

Implementing Locks

The simplest form of synchronization is the mutual exclusion lock (aka Mutex). Anyone who has done concurrent programming on a single machine is familiar with locks, and the same concept can be applied to distributed replicas. Instead of local memory and assembly instructions, these distributed locks can be implemented in terms of the distributed key-value stores described previously.

As with locks in memory, the first step is to acquire the lock:

```
func (Lock l) simpleLock() boolean {
  // compare and swap "1" for "0"
  locked, _ = compareAndSwap(l.lockName, "1", "0")
  return locked
}
```

But of course, it's possible that the lock doesn't already exist, because we are the first to claim it, so we need to handle that case, too:

```
func (Lock l) simpleLock() boolean {
  // compare and swap "1" for "0"
  locked, error = compareAndSwap(l.lockName, "1", "0")
  // lock doesn't exist, try to write "1" with a previous value of
  // non-existent
  if error != nil {
    locked, _ = compareAndSwap(l.lockName, "1", nil)
  }
  return locked
}
```

Traditional lock implementations block until the lock is acquired, so we actually want something like this:

```
func (Lock l) lock() {
  while (!l.simpleLock()) {
    sleep(2)
  }
}
```

This implementation, though simple, has the problem that you will always wait at least a second after the lock is released before you acquire the lock. Fortunately, many key-value stores let you watch for changes instead of polling, so you can implement:

```
func (Lock l) lock() {
  while (!l.simpleLock()) {
    waitForChanges(l.lockName)
  }
}
```

Given this locking function, we can also implement unlock:

```
func (Lock l) unlock() {
  compareAndSwap(l.lockName, "0", "1")
}
```

You might now think that we are done, but remember that we are building this for a distributed system. A process could fail in the middle of holding the lock, and at that point there is no one left to release it. In such a situation, our system will become stuck. To resolve this, we take advantage of the TTL functionality of the key-value store. We change our simpleLock function so that it always writes with a TTL, so if we don't unlock within a given time, the lock will automatically unlock.

```
func (Lock l) simpleLock() boolean {
  // compare and swap "1" for "0"
  locked, error = compareAndSwap(l.lockName, "1", "0", l.ttl)
  // lock doesn't exist, try to write "1" with a previous value of
  // non-existent
  if error != nil {
    locked, _ = compareAndSwap(l.lockName, "1", nil, l.ttl)
  }
  return locked
}
```

When using distributed locks, it is critical to ensure that any processing you do doesn't last longer than the TTL of the lock. One good practice is to set a watchdog timer when you acquire the lock. The watchdog contains an assertion that will crash your program if the TTL of the lock expires before you have called unlock.

By adding TTL to our locks, we have actually introduced a bug into our unlock function. Consider the following scenario:

1. Process-1 obtains the lock with TTL *t*.
2. Process-1 runs really slowly for some reason, for longer than *t*.
3. The lock expires.
4. Process-2 acquires the lock, since Process-1 has lost it due to TTL.
5. Process-1 finishes and calls *unlock*.
6. Process-3 acquires the lock.

At this point, Process-1 believes that it has unlocked the lock that it held at the beginning; it doesn't understand that it has actually lost the lock due to TTL, and in fact unlocked the lock held by Process-2. Then Process-3 comes along and also grabs the lock. Now both Process-2 and Process-3 both believe they own the lock, and hilarity ensues.

Fortunately, the key-value store provides a *resource version* for every write that is performed. Our lock function can store this resource version and augment compareAndSwap to ensure that not only is the value as expected, but the resource version is the same as when the lock operation occurred. This changes our simple Lock function to look like this:

```
func (Lock l) simpleLock() boolean {
  // compare and swap "1" for "0"
  locked, l.version, error = compareAndSwap(l.lockName, "1", "0", l.ttl)
  // lock doesn't exist, try to write "1" with a previous value of
  // non-existent
  if error != null {
    locked, l.version, _ = compareAndSwap(l.lockName, "1", null, l.ttl)
  }
  return locked
}
```

And the unlock function then looks like this:

```
func (Lock l) unlock() {
  compareAndSwap(l.lockName, "0", "1", l.version)
}
```

This ensures that the lock is only unlocked if the TTL has not expired.

Hands On: Implementing Locks in etcd

To implement locks in etcd, you can use a key as the name of the lock and pre-condition writes to ensure that only one lock holder is allowed at a time. For simplicity, we'll use the `etcdctl` command line to lock and unlock the lock. In reality, of course, you would want to use a programming language; there are etcd clients for most popular programming languages.

Let's start by creating a lock named `my-lock`:

```
kubectl exec my-etcd-cluster-0000 -- sh -c \
  "ETCD_API=3 etcdctl --endpoints=${ETCD_ENDPOINTS} set my-lock unlocked"
```

This creates a key in etcd named `my-lock` and sets the initial value to `unlocked`.

Now let's suppose that Alice and Bob both want to take ownership of `my-lock`. Alice and Bob both try to write their name to the lock, using a precondition that the value of the lock is `unlocked`.

Alice first runs:

```
kubectl exec my-etcd-cluster-0000 -- sh -c \
  "ETCD_API=3 etcdctl --endpoints=${ETCD_ENDPOINTS} \
     set --swap-with-value unlocked my-lock alice"
```

And obtains the lock. Now Bob attempts to obtain the lock:

```
kubectl exec my-etcd-cluster-0000 -- sh -c \
  "ETCD_API=3 etcdctl --endpoints=${ETCD_ENDPOINTS} \
     set --swap-with-value unlocked my-lock bob"
Error:  101: Compare failed ([unlocked != alice]) [6]
```

You can see that Bob's attempt to claim the lock has failed, since Alice currently owns the lock.

To unlock the lock, Alice writes `unlocked` with a precondition value of `alice`:

```
kubectl exec my-etcd-cluster-0000 -- sh -c \
  "ETCD_API=3 etcdctl --endpoints=${ETCD_ENDPOINTS} \
     set --swap-with-value alice my-lock unlocked"
```

Implementing Ownership

While locks are great for establishing temporary ownership of some critical component, sometimes you want to take ownership for the duration of the time that the component is running. For example, in a highly available deployment of Kubernetes, there are multiple replicas of the scheduler but only one replica is actively making scheduling decisions. Further, once it becomes the active scheduler, it remains the active scheduler until that process fails for some reason.

Obviously, one way to do this would be to extend the TTL for the lock to a very long period (say a week or longer), but this has the significant downside that if the current lock owner fails, a new lock owner wouldn't be chosen until the TTL expired a week later.

Instead, we need to create a *renewable lock*, which can be periodically renewed by the owner so that the lock can be retained for an arbitrary period of time.

We can extend the existing `Lock` that we defined previously to create a *renewable lock*, which enables the lock holder to renew the lock:

```
func (Lock l) renew() boolean {
  locked, _ = compareAndSwap(l.lockName, "1", "1", l.version, ttl)
  return locked
}
```

Of course, you probably want to do this repeatedly in a separate thread so that you hold onto the lock indefinitely. Notice that the lock is renewed every `ttl/2` seconds; that way there is significantly less risk that the lock will accidentally expire due to timing subtleties:

```
for {
  if !l.renew() {
    handleLockLost()
  }
  sleep(ttl/2)
}
```

Of course, you need to implement the `handleLockLost()` function so that it terminates all activity that required the lock in the first place. In a container orchestration system, the easiest way to do this may simply be to terminate the application and let the orchestrator restart it. This is safe, because some other replica has grabbed the lock in the interim, and when the restarted application comes back online it will become a secondary listener waiting for the lock to become free.

Hands On: Implementing Leases in etcd

To see how we implement leases using etcd, we will return to our earlier locking example and add the `--ttl=<seconds>` flag to our lock create and update calls. The `ttl` flag defines a time after which the lock that we create is deleted. Because the lock disappears after the `ttl` expires, instead of creating with the value of *unlocked*, we will assume that the absence of the lock means that it is unlocked. To do this, we use the `mk` command instead of the `set` command. `etcdctl mk` only succeeds if the key does *not* currently exist.

Thus, to lock a leased lock, Alice executes:

```
kubectl exec my-etcd-cluster-0000 -- \
    sh -c "ETCD_API=3 etcdctl --endpoints=${ETCD_ENDPOINTS} \
        --ttl=10 mk my-lock alice"
```

This creates a leased lock with a duration of 10 seconds.

For Alice to continue to hold the lock, she needs to execute:

```
kubectl exec my-etcd-cluster-0000 -- \
    sh -c "ETCD_API=3 etcdctl --endpoints=${ETCD_ENDPOINTS} \
        set --ttl=10 --swap-with-value alice my-lock alice"
```

It may seem odd that Alice is continually rewriting her own name into the lock, but this is the way the lock lease is extended beyond the 10-second TTL.

If, for some reason, the TTL expires, then the lock update will fail, and Alice will go back to creating the lock using the etcd `mk` command, or Bob may also use the `mk` command to obtain the lock for himself. Bob will likewise need to set and update the lock every 10 seconds to maintain ownership.

Handling Concurrent Data Manipulation

Even with all of the locking mechanisms we have described, it is still possible for two replicas to simultaneously believe they hold the lock for a very brief period of time. To understand how this can happen, imagine that the original lock holder becomes so overwhelmed that its processor stops running for minutes at a time. This can happen on extremely overscheduled machines. In such a case, the lock will time out and some other replica will own the lock. Now the processor frees up the replica that was the original lock holder. Obviously, the `handleLockLost()` function will quickly be called, but there will be a brief period where the replica still believes it holds the lock. Although such an event is fairly unlikely, systems need to be built to be robust to such occurrences. The first step to take is to double-check that the lock is still held, using a function like this:

```
func (Lock l) isLocked() boolean {
  return l.locked && l.lockTime + 0.75 * l.ttl > now()
}
```

If this function executes prior to any code that needs to be protected by a lock, then the probability of two masters being active is significantly reduced, but—it is important to note—it is not completely eliminated. The lock timeout could always occur between the time that the lock was checked and the guarded code was executed. To protect against these scenarios, the system that is being called from the replica needs to validate that the replica sending a request is actually still the master. To do this, the hostname of the replica holding the lock is stored in the key-value store in addition to the state of the lock. That way, others can double-check that a replica asserting that it is the master is in fact the master.

This system diagram is shown in Figure 9-2. In the image, shard2 is the owner of the lock, and when a request is sent to the worker, the worker double-checks with the lock server and validates that shard2 is actually the current owner.

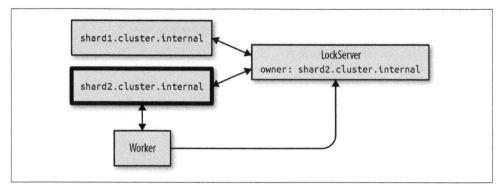

Figure 9-2. A worker double-checking to validate that the requester who sent a message is actually the current owner of the shard

In the second case, shard2 has lost ownership of the lock, but it has not yet realized this so it continues to send requests to the worker node. This time, when the worker node receives a request from shard2, it double-checks with the lock service and realizes that shard2 is no longer the lock owner, and thus the requests are rejected.

To add one final further complicating wrinkle, it's always possible that ownership could be obtained, lost, and then re-obtained by the system, which could actually cause a request to succeed when it should actually be rejected. To understand how this is possible, consider the following sequence of events:

1. Shard-1 obtains ownership to become master.
2. Shard-1 sends a request R1 as master at time T1.
3. The network hiccups and delivery of R1 is delayed.
4. Shard-1 fails TTL because of the network and loses lock to Shard-2.
5. Shard-2 becomes master and sends a request R2 at time T2.
6. Request R2 is received and processed.
7. Shard-2 crashes and loses ownership back to Shard-1.
8. Request R1 finally arrives, and Shard-1 is the current master, so it is accepted, but this is bad because R2 has already been processed.

Such sequences of events seem byzantine, but in reality, in any large system they occur with disturbing frequency. Fortunately, this is similar to the case described previously, which we resolved with the resource version in etcd. We can do the same thing here. In addition to storing the name of the current owner in etcd, we also send the resource version along with each request. So in the previous example, R1 becomes (R1, Version1). Now when the request is received, the double-check validates both the current owner *and* the resource version of the request. If either match fails, the request is rejected. This patches up this example.

## PART III

Batch Computational Patterns

The preceding chapter described patterns for reliable, long-running server applications. This section describes patterns for batch processing. In contrast to long-running applications, batch processes are expected to only run for a short period of time. Examples of a batch process include generating aggregation of user telemetry data, analyzing sales data for daily or weekly reporting, or transcoding video files. Batch processes are generally characterized by the need to process large amounts of data quickly using parallelism to speed up the processing. The most famous pattern for distributed batch processing is the MapReduce pattern, which has become an entire industry in itself. However, there are several other patterns that are useful for batch processing, which are described in the following chapters.

## CHAPTER 10

Work Queue Systems

The simplest form of batch processing is a *work queue*. In a work queue system, there is a batch of work to be performed. Each piece of work is wholly independent of the other and can be processed without any interactions. Generally, the goals of the work queue system are to ensure that each piece of work is processed within a certain amount of time. Workers are scaled up or scaled down to ensure that the work can be handled. An illustration of a generic work queue is shown in Figure 10-1.

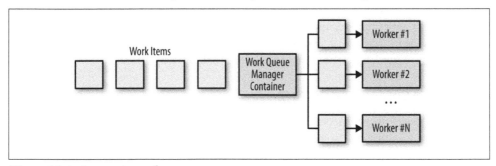

Figure 10-1. A generic work queue

A Generic Work Queue System

The work queue is an ideal way to demonstrate the power of distributed system patterns. Most of the logic in the work queue is wholly independent of the actual work being done, and in many cases the delivery of the work can be performed in an independent manner as well. To illustrate this point, consider the work queue illustrated in Figure 10-1. If we take a look at it again and identify functionality that can be provided by a shared set of *library containers*, it becomes apparent that most of the implementation of a containerized work queue can be shared across a wide variety of users, as shown in Figure 10-2.

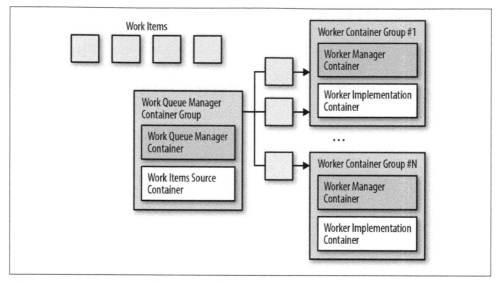

Figure 10-2. The same work queue as shown in Figure 10-1, but this time using reusable containers. The reusable system containers are shown in white while the user-supplied container is shown is grey/blue.

Building a reusable container-based work queue requires the definition of interfaces between the generic library containers and the user-defined application logic. In the containerized work queue, there are two interfaces: the source container interface, which provides a stream of work items that need processing, and the worker container interface, which knows how to actually process a work item.

The Source Container Interface

To operate, every work queue needs a collection of work items that need processing. There are many different sources of work items the work queue, depending on the specific application of the work queue. However, once the set of items has been obtained, the actual operation of the work queue is quite generic. Consequently, we can separate the application-specific queue source logic from the generic queue processing logic. Given the previously defined patterns of container groups, this can be seen as an example of the ambassador pattern defined previously. The generic work queue container is the primary application container, and the application-specific source container is the ambassador that proxies the generic work queue's requests out to the concrete definition of the work queue out in the real world. This container group is illustrated in Figure 10-3.

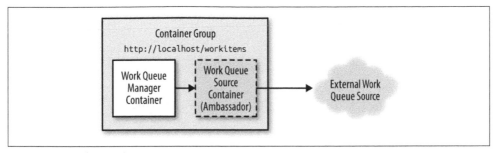

Figure 10-3. The work queue container group

Interestingly, while the ambassador container is clearly application-specific, there is also a variety of generic implementations of the work queue source API. For example, a source might be a list of pictures stored in a cloud storage API, a collection of files stored on network storage, or a queue in an pub/sub system like Kafka or Redis. In these cases, though the user chooses the particular work queue ambassador that fits their scenario, they should be reusing a single generic "library" implementation of the container itself. This minimizes work and maximizes code reuse.

Work queue API

Given this coordination between the generic work-queue manager and the application-specific ambassador, we need a formal definition of the interface between the two containers. Though there are a variety of different protocols, an HTTP REST-ful API is both the easiest to implement as well as the de facto standard for such an interface. The master work queue expects the ambassador to implement the following URLs:

- GET *http://localhost/api/v1/items*
- GET *http://localhost/api/v1/items/<item-name>*

 You might wonder why we include a *v1* in the API definition. Will there ever be a *v2* of this interface? It may not seem logical, but it costs very little to version your API when you initially define it. Refactoring versioning onto an API without it, on the other hand, is very expensive. Consequently, it is a best practice to always add versions to your APIs even if you're not sure they will ever change. Better safe than sorry.

The */items/* URL returns a complete list of all items:

```
{
    kind: ItemList,
    apiVersion: v1,
```

```
    items: [
      "item-1",
      "item-2",
      ….
    ]
}
```

The */items/<item-name>* URL provides the details for a specific item:

```
{
  kind: Item,
  apiVersion: v1,
  data: {
      "some": "json",
    "object": "here",
  }
}
```

Importantly, you will notice that this API doesn't have any affordances for recording that a work item has been processed. We could have designed a more complicated API and then pushed more implementation into the ambassador container, but remember, the goal of this effort is to place as much of the generic implementation inside of the generic work queue manager as possible. To that end, the work queue manager itself is responsible for tracking which items have been processed and which items remain to be processed.

The item details are obtained from this API and the item.data field is passed along to the worker interface for processing.

The Worker Container Interface

Once a particular work item has been obtained by the work queue manager, it needs to be processed by a worker. This is the second container interface in our generic work queue. This container and interface are slightly different than the previous work queue source interface for a few reasons. The first is that it is a one-off API: a single call is made to begin the work, and no other API calls are made throughout the life of the worker container. Secondly, the worker container is not inside a container group with the work queue manager. Instead, it is launched via a container orchestration API and scheduled to its own container group. This means that the work queue manager has to make a remote call to the worker container in order to start work. It also means that we may need to be more careful about security to prevent a malicious user in our cluster from injecting extra work into the system.

With the work queue source API, we used a simple HTTP-based API for sending items back to the work queue manager. This was because we needed to make repeated calls to the API, and security wasn't a concern since everything was running on local-host. With the worker container, we only need to make a single call, and we want to ensure that other users in the system can't accidentally or maliciously add work to our workers. Consequently, for the worker container, we will use a file-based API. Namely, when the worker container is created, it will receive an environment variable named *WORK_ITEM_FILE*; this will point to a file in the container's local filesystem, where the `data` field from a work item has been written to a file. Concretely, as you will see below, this API can be implemented via a Kubernetes `ConfigMap` object that can be mounted into a container group as a file, as illustrated in Figure 10-4.

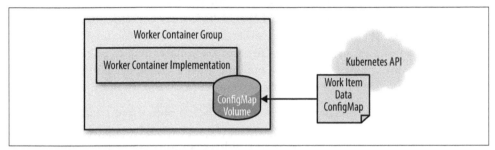

Figure 10-4. The work queue worker API

This file-based API pattern is also easier for the container to implement. Often a work queue worker is simply a shell script across a few command line tools. In that context, spinning up a web server to manage the work to perform is an unnecessary complexity. As was true with the work queue source implementation, most of the worker containers will be special-purpose container images built for specific work queue applications, but there are also generic workers that can be applied to multiple different work queue applications.

Consider the example of a work queue worker that downloads a file from cloud storage and runs a shell script with that file as input, and then copies its output back up to cloud storage. Such a container can be mostly generic but then have the specific script to execute supplied to it as a runtime parameter. In this way, most of the work of file handling can be shared by multiple users/work queues and only the specifics of file processing need to be supplied by the end user.

The Shared Work Queue Infrastructure

Given implementations of the two container interfaces described previously, what is left to implement our reusable work queue implementation? The basic algorithm for the work queue is fairly straightforward:

1. Load the available work by calling into source container interface.

2. Consult with work queue state to determine which work items have been processed or are being processed currently.

3. For these items, spawn jobs that use the worker container interface to process the work item.

4. When one of these worker containers finishes successfully, record that the work item has been completed.

While this algorithm is simple to express in words, it is somewhat more complicated to implement in reality. Fortunately for us, the Kubernetes container orchestrator contains a number of features that make it significantly easier to implement. Namely, Kubernetes contains a `Job` object that allows for the reliable execution of the work queue. The `Job` can be configured to either run the worker container once or to run it until it completes successfully. If the worker container is set to run to completion, then even if a machine in the cluster fails, the job will eventually be run to success. This dramatically simplifies the task of building a work queue because the orchestrator takes on responsibility for the reliable operation of each work item.

Additionally, Kubernetes has annotations for each `Job` object that enable us to mark each job with the work item it is processing. This enables us to understand which items are being processed as well as those that have completed in either failure or success.

Put together, this means that we can implement a work queue on top of the Kubernetes orchestration layer without using any storage of our own.

Thus, the expanded operation of our work queue container looks like this:

Repeat forever

Get the list of work items from the work source container interface.

Get the list of all jobs that have been created to service this work queue.

Difference these lists to find the set of work items that haven't been processed.

For these unprocessed items, create new `Job` objects that spawn the appropriate worker container.

Here is a simple Python script that implements this work queue:

```
import requests
import json
from kubernetes import client, config
import time

namespace = "default"

def make_container(item, obj):
    container = client.V1Container()
    container.image = "my/worker-image"
    container.name = "worker"
    return container
```

```python
def make_job(item):
    response = requests.get("http://localhost:8000/items/{}".format(item))
    obj = json.loads(response.text)
    job = client.V1Job()
    job.metadata = client.V1ObjectMeta()
    job.metadata.name = item
    job.spec = client.V1JobSpec()
    job.spec.template = client.V1PodTemplate()
    job.spec.template.spec = client.V1PodTemplateSpec()
    job.spec.template.spec.restart_policy = "Never"
    job.spec.template.spec.containers = [
        make_container(item, obj)
    ]
    return job

def update_queue(batch):
    response = requests.get("http://localhost:8000/items")

    obj = json.loads(response.text)
    items = obj['items']

    ret = batch.list_namespaced_job(namespace, watch=False)

    for item in items:
        found = False
        for i in ret.items:
            if i.metadata.name == item:
                found = True
        if not found:
            # This function creates the job object, omitted for
            # brevity
            job = make_job(item)
            batch.create_namespaced_job(namespace, job)

config.load_kube_config()
batch = client.BatchV1Api()

while True:
    update_queue(batch)
    time.sleep(10)
```

Hands On: Implementing a Video Thumbnailer

To provide a concrete example of how we might use a work queue, consider the task of generating thumbnails for videos. These thumbnails help users determine which videos they want to watch.

To implement this video thumbnailer, we need two different user containers. The first is the work item source container. The simplest way for this to work is for the work items to appear on a shared disk, such as a Network File System (NFS) share. The work item source simply lists the files in this directory and returns them to the caller. Here's a simple node program that does this:

```
const http = require('http');
const fs = require('fs');

const port = 8080;
const path = process.env.MEDIA_PATH;

const requestHandler = (request, response) => {
        console.log(request.url);
        fs.readdir(path + '/*.mp4', (err, items) => {
                var msg = {
                        'kind': 'ItemList',
                        'apiVersion': 'v1',
                        'items': []
                };
                if (!items) {
                        return msg;
                }
                for (var i = 0; i < items.length; i++) {
                        msg.items.push(items[i]);
                }
                response.end(JSON.stringify(msg));
        });
}

const server = http.createServer(requestHandler);

server.listen(port, (err) => {
        if (err) {
                return console.log('Error starting server', err);
        }

        console.log(`server is active on ${port}`)
});
```

This source of defines the queue of movies to thumbnail. We use the ffmpeg utility to actually perform the thumbnailing work.

You can create a container that uses the following as its command line:

```
ffmpeg -i ${INPUT_FILE} -frames:v 100 thumb.png
```

This command will take one frame every 100 frames (that's the -frames:v 100 flag) and output it as a PNG file (e.g., thumb1.png, thumb2.png, etc.).

You can implement this image processing using an existing ffmpeg Docker image. The jrottenberg/ffmpeg (*https://hub.docker.com/r/jrottenberg/ffmpeg/*) Docker image is a popular choice.

By defining a simple source container as well as an even simpler worker container, we can clearly see the power and utility of a generic, container-based queuing system. It dramatically reduces the time/distance between an idea for implementing a work queue and the corresponding concrete implementation.

Dynamic Scaling of the Workers

The previously described work queue is great for processing work items as quickly as they arrive in the work queue, but this can lead to bursty resource loads being placed onto a container orchestrator cluster. This is good if you have a lot of different workloads that will burst at different times and thus keep your infrastructure evenly utilized. But if you don't have a sufficient number of different workloads, this feast or famine approach to scaling your work queue might require that you over-provision resources to support the bursts that will lay idle (and cost too much money) while you don't have work to perform.

To address this problem, you can limit the overall number of Job objects that your work queue is willing to create. This will naturally serve to limit the number of work items you process in parallel and consequentially limit the maximum amount of resources that you use at a particular time. However, doing this will increase the time to completion (latency) for each work item being completed when under heavy load. If the load is bursty, then this is probably okay because you can use the slack times to catch up with the backlog that developed during a burst of usage. However, if your steady-state usage is too high, your work queue may never be able to catch up and the time to completion will simply get longer and longer.

When your work queue is faced with this situation, you need to have it dynamically adjust itself to increase the parallelism that it is willing to create (and correspondingly the resources it is willing to use) so that it can keep up with the incoming work. Fortunately, there are mathematical formulas that we can use to determine when we need to dynamically scale up our work queue.

Consider a work queue where a new work item arrives an average of once every minute, and each work item takes an average of 30 seconds to complete. Such a system is capable of keeping up with all of the work it receives. Even if a large batch of work arrives all at once and creates a backlog, on average the work queue processes two work items for every one work item that arrives, and thus it will be able to gradually work through its backlog.

If, instead, a new work item arrives on average once every minute and it takes an average of one minute to process each work item, then the system is perfectly balanced, but it does not handle variance well. It can catch up with bursts—but it will take a while, and it has no slack or capacity to absorb a sustained increase in the rate at which new work items arrive. This is probably not an ideal way to run, as some safety margin for growth and other sustained increases in work (or unexpected slow-downs in processing) is needed to preserve a stable system.

Finally, consider a system in which a work item arrives every minute and each item takes 2 minutes to process. In such a system, we are always losing ground. The queue of work will grow without bound and the latency of any one item in the queue will grow toward infinity (and our users will become very frustrated).

Thus, we can keep track of both of these metrics for our work queue, and the average time between work items over an extended period of time (# work items / 24 hours) will give us the *interarrival time* for new work. We can also keep track of the average time to process any one item once we start working on it (not counting any time in the queue). To have a stable work queue, we need to adjust the number of resources so that the time to process any item is less than the interarrival time of new items. If we are processing work items in parallel, we also divide the processing time for a work item by the parallelism. For example, if each item takes one minute to process but we process four items in parallel, the effective time to process one item is 15 seconds, and thus we can sustain an interarrival period of 16 or more seconds.

This approach makes it fairly straightforward to build an autoscaler to dynamically size up our work queue. Sizing down the work queue is somewhat trickier, but you can use the same math as well as a heuristic for the amount of spare capacity for the safety margin you want to maintain. For example, you can reduce the parallelism until the processing time for an item is 90% of the interarrival time for new items.

The Multi-Worker Pattern

One of the themes of this book has been the use of containers for encapsulation and reuse of code. The same holds true for the work queue patterns described in this chapter. In addition to the patterns for reusing containers for driving the work queue itself, you can also reuse multiple different containers to compose a worker implementation. Suppose, for example, that you have three different types of work that you want to perform on a particular work queue item. For example, you might want to detect faces in an image, tag those faces with identities, and then blur the faces in the image. You could write a single worker to perform this complete set of tasks, but this would be a bespoke solution that would not be reusable the next time you want to identify something else, such as cars, yet still provide the same blurring.

To achieve this kind of code reuse, the *multi-worker pattern* is something of a specialization of the adapter pattern described in previous chapters. In this case, the multi-worker pattern transforms a collection of different worker containers into a single unified container that implements the worker interface, yet delegates the actual work to a collection of different, reusable containers. This process is illustrated in Figure 10-5.

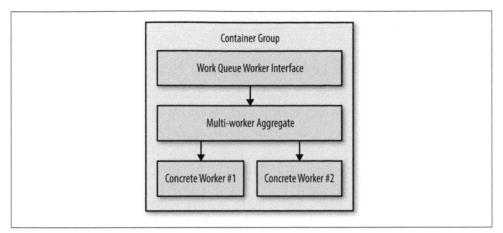

Figure 10-5. The multi-worker aggregator pattern as a group of containers

Because of this code reuse, the composition of multiple different worker containers means an increase in the reuse of code and a reduction in effort for people designing batch-oriented distributed systems.

## CHAPTER 11

Event-Driven Batch Processing

In the previous chapter, we saw a generic framework for work queue processing, as well as a number of example applications of simple work queue processing. Work queues are great for enabling individual transformations of one input to one output. However, there are a number of batch applications where you want to perform more than a single action, or you may need to generate multiple different outputs from a single data input. In these cases, you start to link work queues together so that the output of one work queue becomes the input to one or more other work queues, and so on. This forms a series of processing steps that respond to events, with the events being the completion of the preceding step in the work queue that came before it.

These sort of event-driven processing systems are often called *workflow* systems, since there is a flow of work through a directed, acyclic graph that describes the various stages and their coordination. A basic illustration of such a system is shown in Figure 11-1.

The most straightforward application of this type of system simply chains the output of one queue to the input of the next queue. But as systems become more complicated there are a series of different patterns that emerge for linking a series of work queues together. Understanding and designing in terms of these patterns is important for comprehending how the system is working. The operation of an event-driven batch processor is similar to event-driven FaaS. Consequently, without an overall blueprint for how the different event queues relate to each other, it can be hard to fully understand how the system is operating.

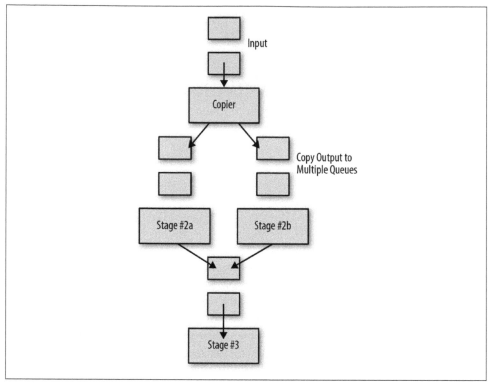

Figure 11-1. This workflow combines copying work into multiple queues (Stage 2a, 2b) parallel processing of those queues, and combining the result back into a single queue (Stage 3)

Patterns of Event-Driven Processing

Beyond the simple work queue described in the previous chapter, there are a number of patterns for linking work queues together. The simplest pattern—one where the output of a single queue becomes the input to a second queue—is straightforward enough that we won't cover it here. We will describe patterns that involve the coordination of multiple different queues or the modification of the output of one or more work queues.

Copier

The first pattern for coordinating work queues is a copier. The job of a copier is to take a single stream of work items and duplicate it out into two or more identical streams. This pattern is useful when there are multiple different pieces of work to be done on the same work item. An example of this might be rendering a video. When rendering a video, there are a variety of different formats that are useful depending on where the video is intended to be shown. There might be a 4K high-resolution format for playing off of a hard drive, a 1080-pixel rendering for digital streaming, a low-resolution format for streaming to mobile users on slow networks, and an animated GIF thumbnail for displaying in a movie-picking user interface. All of these work items can be modeled as separate work queues for each render, but the input to each work item is identical. An illustration of the copier pattern applied to transcoding is shown in Figure 11-2.

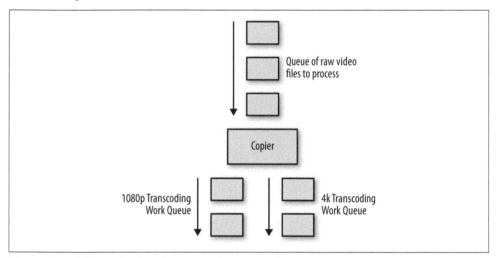

Figure 11-2. The copier batch pattern for transcoding

Filter

The second pattern for event-driven batch processing is a filter. The role of a filter is to reduce a stream of work items to a smaller stream of work items by filtering out work items that don't meet particular criteria. As an example of this, consider setting up a batch workflow that handles new users signing up for a service. Some set of those users will have ticked the checkbox that indicates that they wish to be contacted via email for promotions and other information. In such a workflow, you can filter the set of newly signed-up users to only be those who have explicitly opted into being contacted.

Ideally you would compose a filter work queue source as an ambassador that wraps up an existing work queue source. The original source container provides the complete list of items to be worked on, and the filter container then adjusts that list based on the filter criteria and only returns those filtered results to the work queue infrastructure. An illustration of this use of the adapter pattern is shown in Figure 11-3.

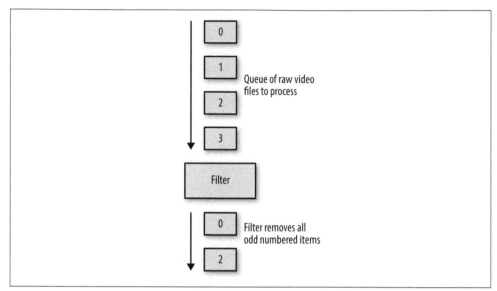

Figure 11-3. An example of a filter pattern that removes all odd-numbered work items

Splitter

Sometimes you don't want to just filter things out by dropping them on the floor, but rather you have two different kinds of input present in your set of work items and you want to divide them into two separate work queues without dropping any of them. For this task, you want to use a splitter. The role of a splitter is to evaluate some criteria—just like a filter—but instead of eliminating input, the splitter sends different inputs to different queues based on that criteria.

An example of an application of the splitter pattern is processing online orders where people can receive shipping notifications either by email or text message. Given a work queue of items that have been shipped, the splitter divides it into two different queues: one that is responsible for sending emails and another devoted to sending text messages. A splitter can also be a copier if it sends the same output to multiple queues, such as when a user selects both text messages and email notifications in the previous example. It is interesting to note that a splitter can actually also be implemented by a copier and two different filters. But the splitter pattern is a more compact representation that captures the job of the splitter more succinctly. An example of using the splitter pattern to send shipping notifications to users is shown in Figure 11-4.

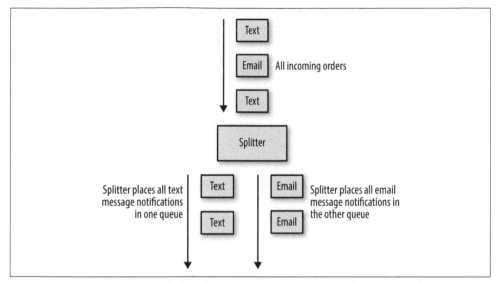

Figure 11-4. An example of the batch splitter pattern splitting shipping notifications into two different queues

Sharder

A slightly more generic form of splitter is a sharder. Much like the sharded server that we saw in earlier chapters, the role of a sharder in a workflow is to divide up a single queue into an evenly divided collection of work items based upon some sort of *sharding function*. There are several different reasons why you might consider sharding your workflow. One of the first is for reliability. If you shard your work queue, then the failure of a single workflow due to a bad update, infrastructure failure, or other problem only affects a fraction of your service.

For example, imagine that you push a bad update to your worker container, which causes your workers to crash and your queue to stop processing work items. If you only have a single work queue that is processing items, then you will have a complete outage for your service with all users affected. If, instead, you have sharded your work queue into four different shards, you have the opportunity to do a staged rollout of your new worker container. Assuming you catch the failure in the first phase of the staged rollout, sharding your queue into four different shards means that only one quarter of your users would be affected.

An additional reason to shard your work queue is to more evenly distribute work across different resources. If you don't really care which region or datacenter is used to process a particular set of work items, you can use a sharder to evenly spread work across multiple datacenters to even out utilization of all datacenters/regions. As with updates, spreading your work queue across multiple failure regions also has the benefit of providing reliability against datacenter or region failures. An illustration of a sharded queue when everything is working correctly is shown in Figure 11-5.

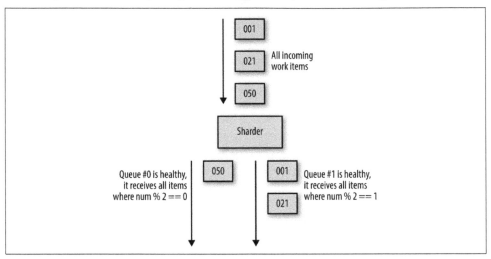

Figure 11-5. An example of the sharding pattern in a healthy operation

When the number of healthy shards is reduced due to failures, the sharding algorithm dynamically adjusts to send work to the remaining healthy work queues, even if only a single queue remains. This is illustrated in Figure 11-6.

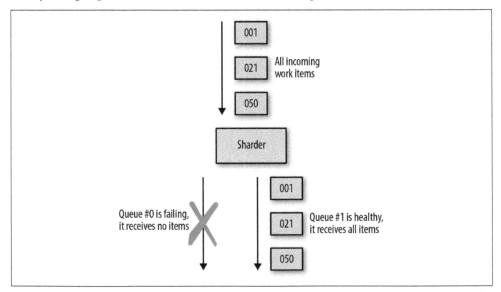

Figure 11-6. When one work queue is unhealthy the remaining work spills over to a different queue

Merger

The last pattern for event-driven or workflow batch systems is a *merger*. A merger is the opposite of a copier; the job of a merger is to take two different work queues and turn them into a single work queue. Suppose, for example, that you have a large number of different source repositories all adding new commits at the same time. You want to take each of these commits and perform a build-and-test for it. It is not scalable to create a separate build infrastructure for each source repository. We can model each of the different source repositories as a separate work queue source that provides a set of commits. We can transform all of these different work queue inputs into a single merged set of inputs using a merger adapter. This merged stream of commits is then the single source to the build system that performs the actual build. The merger is another great example of the adapter pattern, though in this case, the adapter is actually adapting multiple running source containers into a single merged source. This multi-adapter pattern is shown in Figure 11-7.

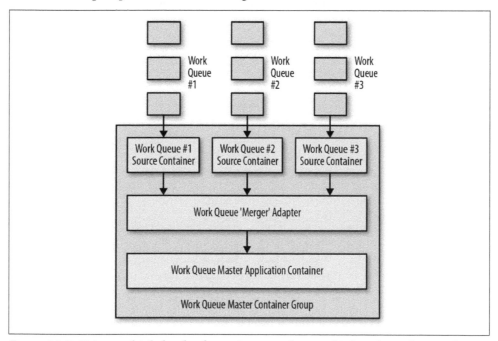

Figure 11-7. Using multiple levels of containers to adapt multiple independent work queues into a single shared queue

Hands On: Building an Event-Driven Flow for New User Sign-Up

A concrete example of a workflow helps show how these patterns can be put together to form a complete operating system. The problem this example will consider is a new-user signup flow.

Imagine that our user acquisition funnel has two stages. The first is user verification. After a new user signs up, the user then has to receive an email notification to validate their email. Once the user validates their email, they are sent a confirmation email. Then they are optionally registered for email, text message, both, or neither for notifications.

The first step in the event-driven workflow is the generation of the verification email. To achieve this reliably, we will use the shard pattern to shard users across multiple different geographic failure zones. This ensures that we will continue to process new user signups, even in the presence of partial failures. Each work queue shard sends a verification email to the end user. At this point, this substage of the workflow is complete. This first stage of the flow is illustrated in Figure 11-8.

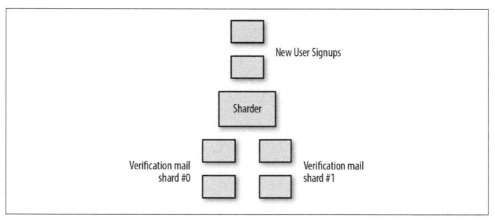

Figure 11-8. The first stage of the workflow for user sign-up

The workflow begins again when we receive a verification email from the end user. These emails become new events in a separate (but clearly related) workflow that sends welcome emails and sets up notifications. The first stage of this workflow is an example of the copier pattern, where the user is copied into two work queues. The first work queue is responsible for sending the welcome email, and the second work queue is responsible for setting up user notifications.

Once the work items have been duplicated between the queues, the email-sending queue simply takes care of sending an email message, and the workflow exits. But remember that because of the use of the copier pattern, there is still an additional copy of the event active in our workflow. This copier triggers an additional work queue to handle notification settings. This work queue feeds into an example of the filter pattern, which splits the work queue into separate email and text message notification queues. These specific queues register the user for email, text, or both notifications.

The remainder of this workflow is shown in Figure 11-9.

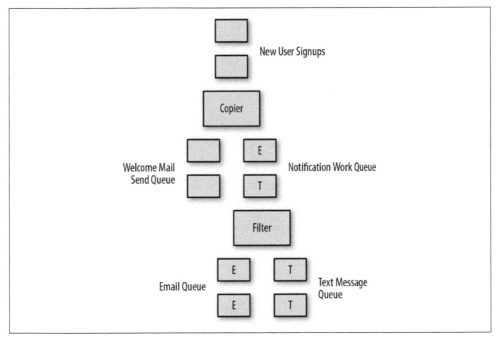

Figure 11-9. The user notification and welcome email work queue

Publisher/Subscriber Infrastructure

We have seen a variety of abstract patterns for linking together different event-driven batch processing patterns. But when it comes time to actually build such a system, we need to figure out how to manage the stream of data that passes through the event-driven workflow. The simplest thing to do would be to simply write each element in the work queue to a particular directory on a local filesystem, and then have each stage monitor that directory for input. But of course doing this with a local filesystem limits our workflow to operating on a single node. We can introduce a network filesystem to distribute files to multiple nodes, but this introduces increasing complexity both in our code and in the deployment of the batch workflow.

Instead, a popular approach to building a workflow like this is to use a publisher/subscriber (pub/sub) API or service. A pub/sub API allows a user to define a collection of queues (sometimes called topics). One or more *publishers* publishes messages to these queues. Likewise, one or more *subscribers* is listening to these queues for new messages. When a message is published, it is reliably stored by the queue and subsequently delivered to subscribers in a reliable manner.

At this point, most public clouds feature a pub/sub API such as Azure's EventGrid or Amazon's Simple Queue Service. Additionally, the open source Kafka project (*https:// kafka.apache.org*) provides a very popular pub/sub implementation that you can run on your own hardware as well as on cloud virtual machines. For the remainder of this overview of pub/sub APIs we'll use Kafka for our examples, but they are relatively simple to port to alternate pub/sub APIs.

Hands On: Deploying Kafka

There are obviously many ways to deploy Kafka, and one of the easiest ways is to run it as a container using a Kubernetes cluster and the Helm package manager.

Helm is a package manager for Kubernetes that makes it easy to deploy and manage prepackaged, off-the-shelf applications like Kafka. If you don't already have the `helm` command line tool installed, you can install it from *https://helm.sh*.

Once the `helm` tool is on your machine, you need to initialize it. Initializing Helm deploys a cluster-side component named `tiller` to your cluster and installs some templates to your local filesystem:

```
helm init
```

Now that helm is initialized, you can install Kafka using this command:

```
helm repo add incubator http://storage.googleapis.com/kubernetes-charts-incubator
helm install --name kafka-service incubator/kafka
```

Helm templates have different levels of production hardening and support. `stable` templates are the most strictly vetted and supported, whereas `incubator` templates like Kafka are more experimental and have less production mileage. Regardless, incubator templates are useful for quick proof of concepts as well as a place to start from when implementing a production deployment of a Kubernetes-based service.

Once you have Kafka up and running, you can create a topic to publish to. Generally in batch processing, you're going to use a topic to represent the output of one module in your workflow. This output is likely to be the input for another module in the workflow.

For example, if you are using the Sharder pattern described previously, you would have a topic for each of the output shards. If you called your output Photos and you chose to have three shards, then you would have three topics: Photos-1, Photos-2, and Photos-3. Your sharder module would output messages to the appropriate topic, after applying the sharding function.

Here's how you create a topic. First, create a container in the cluster so that we can access Kafka:

```
for x in 0 1 2; do
  kubectl run kafka --image=solsson/kafka:0.11.0.0 --rm --attach --command -- \
    ./bin/kafka-topics.sh --create --zookeeper kafka-service-zookeeper:2181 \
      --replication-factor 3 --partitions 10 --topic photos-$x
done
```

Note that there are two interesting parameters in addition to the topic name and the zookeeper service. They are --replication-factor and --partitions. The replication factor is how many different machines messages in the topic will be replicated to. This is the redundancy that is available in case things crash. A value of 3 or 5 is recommended. The second parameter is the number of partitions for the topic. The number of partitions represents the maximum distribution of the topic onto multiple machines for purposes of load balancing. In this case, since there are 10 partitions, there can be at most 10 different replicas of the topic for load balancing.

Now that we have created a topic, we can send messages to that topic:

```
kubectl run kafka-producer --image=solsson/kafka:0.11.0.0 --rm -it --command -- \
    ./bin/kafka-console-producer.sh --broker-list kafka-service-kafka:9092 \
    --topic photos-1
```

Once that command is up and connected, you should see the Kafka prompt and you can then send messages to the topic(s). To receive messages, you can run:

```
kubectl run kafka-consumer --image=solsson/kafka:0.11.0.0 --rm -it --command -- \
    ./bin/kafka-console-consumer.sh --bootstrap-server kafka-service-kafka:9092\
    --topic photos-1 \
        --from-beginning
```

Of course, running these command lines only gives you a taste of how to communicate via Kafka messages. To build a real-world event-driven batch processing system, you would likely use a proper programming language and Kafka SDK to access the service. But on the other hand, never underestimate the power of a good Bash script!

This section has shown how installing Kafka into your Kubernetes cluster can dramatically simplify the task of building a work queue based system.

Coordinated Batch Processing

The previous chapter described a number of patterns for splitting and chaining queues together to achieve more complex batch processing. Duplicating and producing multiple different outputs is often an important part of batch processing, but sometimes it is equally important to pull multiple outputs back together in order to generate some sort of aggregate output. A generic illustration of such a pattern is shown in Figure 12-1.

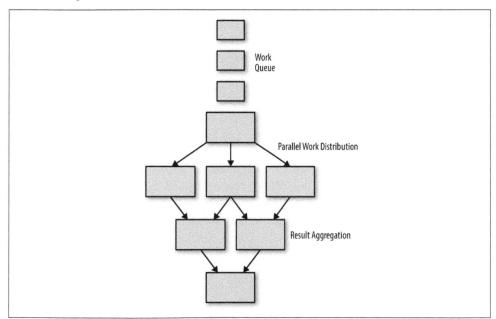

Figure 12-1. A generic parallel work distribution and result aggregation batch system

Probably the most canonical example of this aggregation is the *reduce* part of the MapReduce pattern. It's easy to see that the map step is an example of sharding a work queue, and the reduce step is an example of coordinated processing that eventually reduces a large number of outputs down to a single aggregate response. However, there are a number of different aggregate patterns for batch processing, and this chapter discusses a number of them in addition to real-world applications.

Join (or Barrier Synchronization)

In previous chapters, we saw patterns for breaking up work and distributing it in parallel on multiple nodes. In particular, we saw how a sharded work queue could distribute work in parallel to a number of different work queue shards. However, sometimes when processing a workflow, it is necessary to have the complete set of work available to you before you move on to the next stage of the workflow.

One option for doing this was shown in the previous chapter, which was to merge multiple queues together. However, merge simply blends the output of two work queues into a single work queue for additional processing. While the merge pattern is sufficient in some cases, it does not ensure that a complete dataset is present prior to the beginning of processing. This means that there can be no guarantees about the completeness of the processing being performed, as well as no opportunity to compute aggregate statistics for all of the elements that have been processed.

Instead, we need a stronger, coordinated primitive for batch data processing, and that primitive is the *join* pattern. Join is similar to joining a thread. The basic idea is that all of the work is happening in parallel, but work items aren't released out of the join until all of the work items that are processed in parallel are completed. This is also generally known as *barrier* synchronization in concurrent programming. An illustration of the join pattern for a coordinated batch is shown in Figure 12-2.

Coordination through join ensures that no data is missing before some sort of aggregation phase is performed (e.g., finding the sum of some value in a set). The value of the join is that it ensures that all of the data in the set is present. The downside of the join pattern is that it requires that all data be processed by a previous stage before subsequent computation can begin. This reduces the parallelism that is possible in the batch workflow, and thus increases the overall latency of running the workflow.

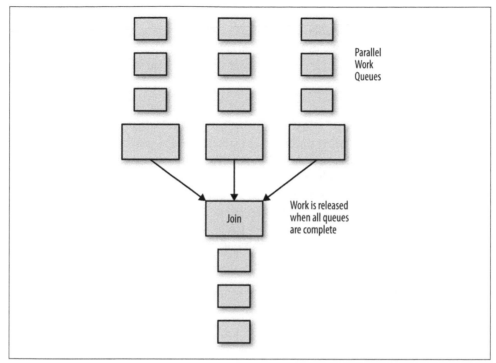

Figure 12-2. The join pattern for batch processing

Reduce

If sharding a work queue is an example of the *map* phase of the canonical map/reduce algorithm, then what remains is the *reduce* phase. Reduce is an example of a coordinated batch processing pattern because it can happen regardless of how the input is split up, and it is used similar to *join*; that is, to group together the parallel output of a number of different batch operations on different pieces of data.

However, in contrast to the join pattern described previously, the goal of reduce is not to wait until all data has been processed, but rather to optimistically merge together all of the parallel data items into a single comprehensive representation of the full set.

With the reduce pattern, each step in the reduce merges several different outputs into a single output. This stage is called "reduce" because it reduces the total number of outputs. Additionally, it reduces the data from a complete data item to simply the representative data necessary for producing the answer to a specific batch computation. Because the reduce phase operates on a range of input, and produces a similar output, the reduce phase can be repeated as many or as few times as necessary in order to successfully reduce the output down to a single output for the entire data set.

This is a fortunate contrast to the join pattern, because unlike join, it means that reduce can be started in parallel while there is still processing going on as part of the map/shard phase. Of course, in order to produce a complete output, all of the data must be processed eventually, but the ability to begin early means that the batch computation executes more quickly overall.

Hands On: Count

To understand how the reduce pattern works, consider the task of counting the number of instances of a particular word in a book. We can first use sharding to divide up the work of counting words into a number of different work queues. As an example, we could create 10 different sharded work queues with 10 different people responsible for counting words in each queue. We can shard the book among these 10 work queues by looking at the page number. All pages that end in the number 1 will go to the first queue, all pages that end in the number 2 will go to the second, and so forth.

Once all of the people have finished processing their pages, they write down their results on a piece of paper. For example, they might write:

```
a: 50
the: 17
cat: 2
airplane: 1
...
```

This can be output to the reduce phase. Remember that the reduce pattern reduces by combining two or more outputs into a single output.

Given a second output:

```
a: 30
the: 25
dog: 4
airplane: 2
...
```

The reduction proceeds by summing up all of the counts for the various words, in this example producing:

```
a: 80
the 42
dog: 4
cat: 2
airplane: 3
...
```

It's clear to see that this reduction phase can be repeated on the output of previous reduce phases until there is only a single reduced output left. This is valuable since this means that reductions can be performed in parallel.

Ultimately, in this example you can see that the output of the reduction will be a single output with the count of all of the various words that are present in the book.

Sum

A similar but slightly different form of reduction is the summation of a collection of different values. This is like counting, but rather than simply counting one for every value, you actually add together a value that is present in the original output data.

Suppose, for example, you want to sum the total population of the United States. Assume that you will do this by measuring the population in every town and then summing them all together.

A first step might be to shard the work into work queues of towns, sharded by state. This is a great first sharding, but it's clear that even when distributed in parallel, it would take a single person a long time to count the number of people in every town. Consequently, we perform a second sharding to another set of work queues, this time by county.

At this point, we have parallelized first to the level of states, then to the level of counties, and then each work queue in each county produces a stream of outputs of (town, population) tuples.

Now that we are producing output, the reduce pattern can kick in.

In this case, the reduce doesn't even really need to be aware of the two-level sharding that we performed. It is sufficient for the reduce to simply grab two or more output items, such as (`Seattle, 4,000,000`) and (`Northampton, 25,000`), and sum them together to produce a new output (`Seattle-Northampton, 4,025,000`). It's clear to see that, like counting, this reduction can be performed an arbitrary number of times with the same code running at each interval, and at the end, there will only be a single output containing the complete population of the United States. Importantly, again, nearly all of the computation required is happening in parallel.

Histogram

As a final example of the reduce pattern, consider that while we are counting the population of the United States via parallel sharding/mapping and reducing, we also want to build a model of the average American family. To do this, we want to develop a *histogram* of family size; that is, a model that estimates the total number of families with zero to 10 children. We will perform our multi-level sharding exactly as before (indeed, we can likely use the same workers).

However, this time, the output of the data collection phase is a histogram per town.

```
0: 15%
1: 25%
2: 50%
3: 10%
4: 5%
```

From the previous examples, we can see that if we apply the reduce pattern, we should be able to combine all of these histograms to develop a comprehensive picture of the United States. At first blush, it may seem quite difficult to understand how to merge these histograms, but when combined with the population data from the summation example, we can see that if we multiply each histogram by its relative population, then we can obtain the total population for each item being merged. If we then divide this new total by the sum of the merged populations, it is clear that we can merge and update multiple different histograms into a single output. Given this, we can apply the reduce pattern as many times as necessary until a single output is produced.

Hands On: An Image Tagging and Processing Pipeline

To see how coordinated batch processing can be used to accomplish a larger batch task, consider the job of tagging and processing a set of images. Let us assume that we have a large collection of images of highways at rush hour, and we want to count both the numbers of cars, trucks, and motorcycles, as well as distribution of the colors of each of the cars. Let us also suppose that there is a preliminary step to blur the license plates of all of the cars to preserve anonymity.

The images are delivered to us as a series of HTTPS URLs where each URL points to a raw image. The first stage in the pipeline is to find and blur the license plates. To simplify each task in the work queue, we will have one worker that detects a license plate, and a second worker that blurs that location in the image. We will combine these two different worker containers into a single container group using the multi-worker pattern described in the previous chapter. This separation of concerns may seem unnecessary, but it is useful given that the workers for blurring images can be reused to blur other outputs (e.g., people's faces).

Additionally, to ensure reliability and to maximize parallel processing, we will shard the images across multiple worker queues. This complete workflow for sharded image blurring is shown in Figure 12-3.

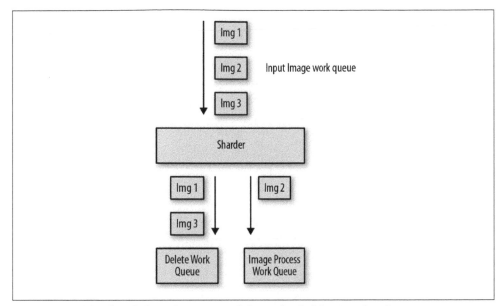

Figure 12-3. The sharded work queue and the multiple blurring shards

Once each image has been successfully blurred, we will upload it to a different location, and we will then delete the originals. However, we don't want to delete the original until *all* of the images have been successfully blurred in case there is some sort of catastrophic failure and we need to rerun this entire pipeline. Thus, to wait for all of the blurring to complete, we use the join pattern to merge the output of all of the sharded blurring work queues into a single queue that will only release its items after all of the shards have completed the work.

Now we are ready to delete the original images as well as begin work on car model and color detection. Again, we want to maximize the throughput of this pipeline, so we will use the copier pattern from the previous chapter to duplicate the work queue items to two different queues:

- A work queue that deletes the original images
- A work queue that identifies the type of vehicle (car, truck, motorcycle) and the color of the vehicle

Figure 12-4 shows these stages of the processing pipeline.

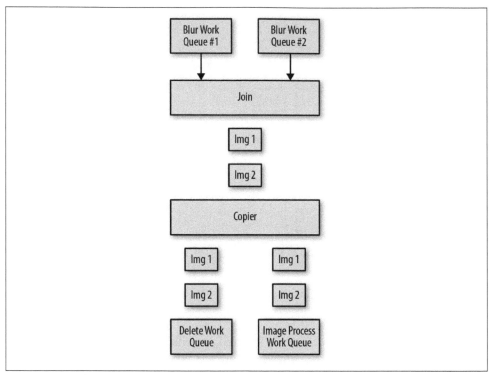

Figure 12-4. The output join, copier, deletion, and image recognition parts of the pipeline

Finally we need to design the queue that identifies vehicles and colors and aggregates these statistics into a final count. To do this, we first again apply the shard pattern to distribute the work out to a number of queues. Each of these queues has two different workers: one that identifies the location and type of each vehicle and one that identifies the color of a region. We will again join these together using the multi-worker pattern described in the previous chapter. As before, the separation of code into different containers enables us to reuse the color detection container for multiple tasks beyond identifying the color of the cars.

The output of this work queue is a JSON tuple that looks like this:

```
{
  "vehicles": {
    "car": 12,
    "truck": 7,
    "motorcycle": 4
  },
  "colors": {
    "white": 8,
    "black": 3,
    "blue": 6,
    "red": 6
```

```
    }
  }
```

This data represents the information found in a single image. To aggregate all of this data together, we will use the reduce pattern described previously and made famous by MapReduce to sum everything together just as we did in the count example above. At the end, this reduce pipeline stage produces the final count of images and colors found in the complete set of images.

## CHAPTER 13

Conclusion: A New Beginning?

Every company, regardless of its origins, is becoming a digital company. This transformation requires the delivery of APIs and services to be consumed by mobile applications, devices in the internet of things (IoT), or even autonomous vehicles and systems. The increasing criticality of these systems means that it is necessary for these online systems to be built for redundancy, fault tolerance, and high availability. At the same time, the requirements of business necessitate rapid agility to develop and roll out new software, iterate on existing applications, or experiment with new user interfaces and APIs. The confluence of these requirements has led to an order of magnitude increase in the number of distributed systems that need to be built.

The task of building these systems is still far too difficult. The overall cost of developing, updating, and maintaining such a system is far too high. Likewise, the set of people with the capabilities and skills to build such applications is far too small to address the growing need.

Historically, when these situations presented themselves in software development and technology, new abstraction layers and patterns of software development emerged to make building software faster, easier, and more reliable. This first occurred with the development of the first compilers and programming languages. Later, the development of object-oriented programming languages and managed code occurred. Likewise, at each of these moments, these technical developments crystallized the distillation of the knowledge and practices of experts into a series of algorithms and patterns that could be applied by a much wider group of practitioners. Technological advancement combined with the establishment of patterns democratized the process of developing software and expanded the set of developers who could build applications on the new platform. This in turn led to the development of more applications and application diversity, which in turn expanded the market for these developer's skills.

Again, we find ourselves at a moment of technological transformation. The need for distributed systems far exceeds our ability to deliver them. Fortunately, the development of technology has produced another set of tools to further expand the pool of developers capable of building these distributed systems. The recent development of containers and container orchestration has brought tools that enable rapid, easier development of distributed systems. With luck, these tools, when combined with the patterns and practices described in this book, can enhance and improve the distributed systems built by current developers, and more importantly develop a whole new expanded group of developers capable of building these systems.

Patterns like sidecars, ambassadors, sharded services, FaaS, work queues, and more can form the foundation on which modern distributed systems are built. Distributed system developers should no longer be building their systems from scratch as individuals but rather collaborating together on reusable, shared implementations of canonical patterns that form the basis of all of the systems we collectively deploy. This will enable us to meet the demands of today's reliable, scalable APIs and services and empower a new set of applications and services for the future.

Index

nginx server
  as ambassador, 27-29
  SSL-terminating, 55-56

O

object-oriented programming, patterns for, 3
open source software, 3
ownership election, 93-105
  (see also master election)
  determining need for master election, 94
  handling concurrent data manipulation,
    103-105
  master election basics, 95-103

P

PaaS (see platform as a service)
parameterized sidecar containers, 17
patterns, 2-4
  (see also specific types, e.g.: container pat-
    terns)
  as collection of best practices, 4
  as shared language, 5
  defined, 4
  event-driven batch processing systems,
    122-127
  for FaaS, 84-91
  formalization of algorithmic programming,
    3
  identifying shared components with, 5
  object-oriented programming and, 3
  open source software and, 3
  value of, 4-6
pipelines (see event-based pipelines)
platform as a service (PaaS), 15
pod, 9
pricing, FaaS and, 84
Prometheus, 33
publisher/subscriber API, 129
Python
  decorator pattern, 85

R

rate limiting, 54
readiness probes, 46
Redis
  and adapter pattern, 33, 35
  sharded, 23-25
reduce pattern, 135

(see also MapReduce pattern)
renewable lock, 102
replicated load-balanced services, 45-57
  application-layer services, 49
  creating a service in Kubernetes, 47
  expanding the caching layer, 53-57
  introducing a caching layer, 49-53
  readiness probes for load balancing, 46
  session tracked services, 48
  stateless services, 45-48
request decorator, 85
request splitting
  ambassador patterns for, 26-29
  implementing 10% experiments, 27-29
request-based processing, FaaS and, 84
requests, events vs., 87
resource isolation, 7
resource version, 100
response decorator, 85
root (load-balancing node), 59

S

scaling
  assignment (see ownership election)
  cache, 50
  consistent hashing function and, 49
  FaaS, 84
  horizontal, 46
  hot sharding systems and, 70
  microservice decoupling and, 42
  scatter/gather pattern (see scatter/gather
    pattern)
  sharding (see sharded services)
  straggler problem, 78
  teams, 8
scatter/gather pattern, 73-80
  distributed document search, 75
  leaf sharding, 76-79
  root distribution, 74
  scaling for reliability and scale, 79
separation of concerns
  ambassador pattern, 23
  containerization, 8
serverless computing, FaaS vs., 81
service broker, defined, 25
service brokering, ambassador for, 25
service discovery, 25
serving patterns

About the Author

Brendan Burns is a distinguished engineer at Microsoft and a cofounder of the Kubernetes open source project. At Microsoft he works on Azure, focusing on Containers and DevOps. Prior to Microsoft, he worked at Google in the Google Cloud Platform, where he helped build APIs like Deployment Manager and Cloud DNS. Before working on cloud computing, he worked on Google's web-search infrastructure, with a focus on low-latency indexing. He has a PhD in computer science from the University of Massachusetts Amherst with a specialty in robotics. He lives in Seattle with his wife, Robin Sanders, their two children, and a cat, Mrs. Paws, who rules over their household with an iron paw.

Colophon

The animal on the cover of *Designing Distributed Systems* is a Java sparrow. This bird is loathed in the wild but loved in captivity. The Java's scientific name is *Padda oryzivora*. Padda stands for paddy, the method of cultivating rice, and Oryza is the genus for domestic rice. Therefore, *Padda oryzivora* means "rice paddy eater." Farmers destroy thousands of wild Javas each year to prevent the flocks from devouring their crops. They also trap the birds for food or sell them in the international bird trade. Despite this battle, the species continues to thrive in Java and Bali in Indonesia, as well as Australia, Mexico, and North America.

Its plumage is pearly-grey, turning pinkish on the front and white towards the tail. It has a black head with white cheeks. Its large bill, legs, and eye circles are bright pink. The song of the Java sparrow begins with single notes, like a bell, before developing into a continuous trilling and clucking, mixed with high-pitched and deeper notes.

The main part of their diet is rice, but they also eat small seeds, grasses, insects, and flowering plants. In the wild, these birds will build a nest out of dried grass normally under the roofs of buildings or in bushes or treetops. The Java will lay a clutch of three or four eggs between February to August, with most eggs laid in April or May.

Its striking plumage, enchanting sounds, and ease of care create a demand for these birds in the cage-bird trade. Conservation efforts are underway to ensure that the market demand is met by captive-bred birds rather than wild caught.

Many of the animals on O'Reilly covers are endangered; all of them are important to the world. To learn more about how you can help, go to *animals.oreilly.com*.

The cover image is from *Lydekker's Royal Natural History*. The cover fonts are URW Typewriter and Guardian Sans. The text font is Adobe Minion Pro; the heading font is Adobe Myriad Condensed; and the code font is Dalton Maag's Ubuntu Mono.

Learn from experts.
Find the answers you need.

Sign up for a **10-day free trial** to get **unlimited access** to all of the content on Safari, including Learning Paths, interactive tutorials, and curated playlists that draw from thousands of ebooks and training videos on a wide range of topics, including data, design, DevOps, management, business—and much more.

Start your free trial at:
oreilly.com/safari

(No credit card required.)

Milton Keynes UK
Ingram Content Group UK Ltd.
UKHW050359220924
448614UK00002BA/11